THE COTTAGE GARDEN

THE COTTAGE GARDEN

Margery Fish at East Lambrook Manor

Susan Chivers and Suzanne Woloszynska
Photographs by Peter Woloszynski

JOHN MURRAY

© Susan Chivers and Suzanne Woloszynska (text)
All contemporary photographs © Peter Woloszynski
First published in 1990
by John Murray (Publishers) Ltd
50 Albemarle Street, London W1X 4BD

British Library Cataloguing in Publication Data

Chivers, Susan
    The cottage garden: Margery Fish at East Lambrook Manor.
    1. England. Cottages. Gardens
    I. Title   II. Woloszynska, Suzanne
    712.60942

ISBN 0-7195-4790-3

Typeset and printed by Butler & Tanner Ltd,
Frome and London

Contents

Acknowledgements   vii

Introduction   ix

1 Margery Fish's Early Life   1

2 Margery Fish and Cottage Gardening   11

3 Influences on Margery Fish   23

4 The Making of Margery Fish's Garden   32

5 The Mature Garden in Winter and Spring   50

6 The Mature Garden in Summer   68

7 The Mature Garden in Late Summer and Autumn   89

8 The Garden Today   102

Appendix: Margery Fish's Writing   114

Index   117

The colour plates appear between pages 50 and 51

Acknowledgements

WHILE RESEARCHING this book we have been touched by the tremendous encouragement and kindness we have received from many of Mrs Fish's friends and colleagues.

We are especially grateful to Henry Boyd-Carpenter (Mrs Fish's nephew) and to Andrew Norton (the present owner of East Lambrook Manor) for their unstinting enthusiasm and co-operation and for giving us unlimited access to their records. Our warm thanks also to the following, all of whom took much time and trouble to recall their impressions of Mrs Fish and her garden: Barry Ambrose, Molly Anderson, Marjorie Bitterling, David and Joy Broomfield, Elizabeth Bond, Christopher Brickell, Jean Burgess, Charles Clive-Ponsonby-Fane, John Codrington, Dame Sylvia Crowe, Valerie Finnis, Jean Goscomb, Pam Gossage, Arthur Hellyer, Anthony Huxley, Christopher Lloyd, Sheila McQueen, Esther Merton, the late James Platt, Philippa Rakusen, Anne Scott-James, Eileen Southcombe, Netta Statham, Graham Stuart Thomas, Derek Tilley, Michael Wallis and Maureen Whitty.

We are also grateful to the Fellows who kindly responded to our letter about Mrs Fish in the Journal of the Royal Horticultural Society. We regret that lack of space prevented us from using more of their anecdotes.

Our sincere thanks also to Dr Anthony Lord for his invaluable help in checking the plant names in the text and to our editor, Patrick Taylor who has guided us through the production of this book with such unfailing good advice and patience. We must also thank Faber & Faber for kind permission to quote from Margery Fish's books.

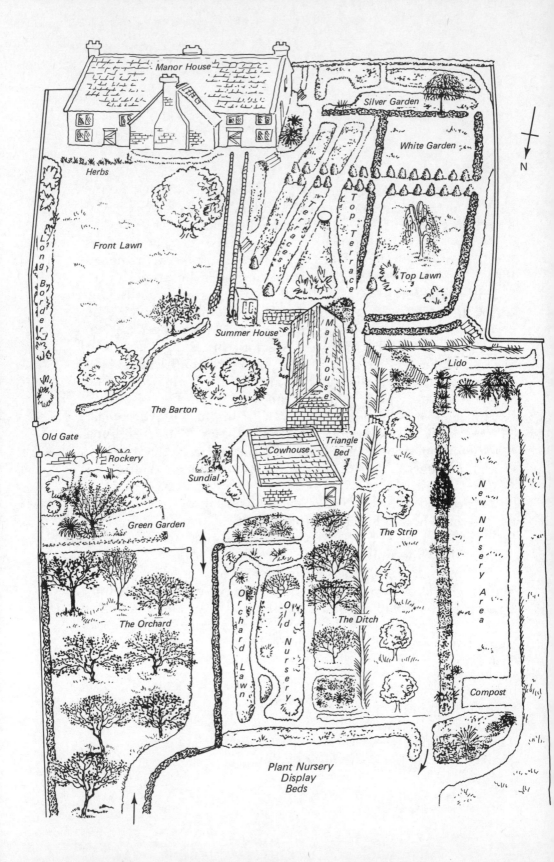

Introduction

A T DIFFERENT MOMENTS in garden history certain gardens catch the imagination and seem to be distinctive of that time. The garden that Margery Fish made at East Lambrook Manor in Somerset between 1938 and her death in 1969 is certainly an example. John Sales of the National Trust wrote of it in 1980, 'In the development of gardening in the second half of the twentieth-century no garden has yet had greater effect.' The reasons for this impact are various. First, Mrs Fish was a remarkable person as we shall show in our brief life of her. Second, she was a brilliant advocate – in writing and lecturing – of her gardening ideas. Third, and most important of all, the style of gardening that she contrived was so completely in tune with the times. She realised that the days of comfortable middle-class gardening, in which a paid gardener did all the work, were doomed. When she started gardening, immediately before World War II, cheap labour was plentiful; after the war it was scarcely to be found. A new kind of garden was needed in which owners played a vital part, often doing all the gardening themselves and taking an intense and increasingly informed interest in it. A less formal garden, which was much less burdensome in terms of labour, met the need.

Mrs Fish saw this informality as having its origins in a sort of idealised cottage garden with, certainly, hollyhocks nodding at the gate. But its origins went much deeper than that, to the same ideas as those which influenced the natural gardening philosophy of William Robinson. Part of that philosophy was the idea that a hardy plant, in the right site, would to a large extent look after itself. Although it had never been spelt out in that way, this had also been the cottagers' belief. Who has not envied in some untidy cottage garden an annoyingly healthy clump of some desirable plant, Madonna lilies for example, which has stubbornly refused to perform in one's own garden?

When Mrs Fish started gardening the cottage garden was still a living tradition. She was one of the first to recognise that these gardens were a priceless repository of plants which survived only because of the cottagers' slow-changing conservatism. In her own lifetime she saw many of these plants become increasingly rare and realised that they would be lost forever unless there was some conscious effort to preserve them. Many have been lost, and continue to be lost, but her own efforts played a large part in starting the movement for the conservation of garden plants.

By the time Mrs Fish started gardening other gardens had already been strongly influenced by the cottage garden tradition – for example Hidcote and Sissinghurst. But, although the owners of those gardens certainly gardened themselves, their gardens were on a grand scale and depended on paid gardeners. East Lambrook was on a much more domestic scale and it was this that enabled Mrs Fish's admirers so easily to understand what she was doing and to relate it to their own gardening experiences. Her ideas and her style of gardening still have a seductive power. Above all the garden she made at East Lambrook gloriously survives so that visitors may see her ideas in practice and, once more, fall under her spell.

Margery Fish's
Early Life

WHEN IN THE summer of 1911, a young woman left Clark's College of Chancery Lane, London, an establishment which advertised itself as preparing its secretarial students for the Civil Service, the professions and business, she took with her a glowing reference: 'It is a pleasure to recommend Miss Margery Townshend to any employer who requires a sensible, well-educated and smart citizen. She has a wonderful capacity for work; she applies herself diligently and zealously to everything she takes up. She has a good command of English which makes her a good correspondent. It rarely falls to my lot to recommend so excellent a student and one who has reached such a high mark in all the subjects of our curriculum. I am certain of her success.'

The reference was as prophetic as it was accurate, but its author could not have known that this talented and conscientious young secretary would achieve success in a field far removed from the commercial world. Margery Fish (née Townshend), perhaps one of the most influential English gardeners of the century, went on to apply herself 'diligently and zealously' to everything she tackled throughout her life, whether it was work or pleasure. She never did anything in a half-hearted way. Later in life, her skill as a correspondent stood her in good stead when she took to writing. Her legacy of gardening books and articles, many considered to be indispensable to a keen gardener, bear witness to her talent. And she retained that prodigious capacity for work into old age.

To within days of her death, her self-discipline was still evident as she kept to the strict working regime that had been the pattern of her life for many years. It was her rule to take breakfast at nine and then work on her voluminous correspondence. From her desk she went into the garden where she worked, without interruption, until a quarter past one when she took lunch. Then back in the garden until about six when supper was served. If the light permitted, she returned to the garden until darkness drove her indoors when she would resume work on her books or articles, often writing until one or two in the morning. It was a punishing schedule and would have exhausted many younger women, but Mrs Fish appeared to thrive on it. Even when suffering from the minor ailments of old age, she never complained, working with a determination that, at times, made life trying for the people around her. She could be an exacting employer, expecting her staff to work with the same devotion and discipline as herself.

In old age, she looked the epitome of the English country-woman. Of average height and stoutly built, she liked to dress in thick tweeds in winter and simple Liberty-print dresses in summer. She gave the impression of someone who did not care about clothes but they were well-cut and her shoes were specially made for her in London. It was her custom to wear her grey hair in a bun and this, combined with her 'sensible' shoes, gave her a somewhat austere appearance that belied her sense of fun and kindness. This 'countrywoman image' could not have been more different from the way she looked in her youth. Then, according to her nephew, Henry Boyd-Carpenter, she was very good-looking and, like most young women, took a great deal of trouble over her appearance. London was her home then and she had a responsible job that demanded she look smart at all times. It was only in late middle age that she cared less about how she looked, simply because she was too busy with her garden, writing and lecturing. Jean Goscomb, who came to work for Mrs Fish in 1965, recalls her first impression on meeting her future employer: 'This well-built woman was wearing a very faded green corduroy skirt with the hem hanging down at the back and an even more faded green jacket. A little stitched tweed hat sat on the top of wispy grey hair, and she wore thick lisle stockings and brogues on rather large feet. She was carrying a trug full of weeds in one hand and a small fork in the other ... When she was working in the garden that was the way she dressed in the clothes in which she felt happiest and it did not matter who was coming . . . Her personality was such that you were only aware of her low strong voice and her commanding figure.'

Unlike some other notable English gardeners – Vita Sackville-West and Christopher Lloyd, for example – Mrs Fish was not raised in the depths of the country. Although her parents were keen gardeners, their interest did not rub off on the young Margery and, later in life, she confessed to the writer and gardener Dawn Macleod that she might have learned a lot from her parents, but resented being used as on-the-spot labour. 'You can't really be keen on gardening until you have one of your own. Doing as you are told in other people's gardens is a bore.'

She was born in 1892 in Enfield, then an affluent London suburb, to Florence Buttfield and Ernest Townshend, a tea broker in Mark Lane. She was the second of four daughters, all of whom were intelligent and accomplished but who displayed traits for free thinking and lively humour that must at times have dismayed their strait-laced parents. Her early life was comfortably conventional but strictly disciplined in the way of middle class families of the time. The sisters were close and enjoyed each others' company. Indeed, familial affection was important to Mrs Fish all her life; she spoke daily on the telephone to her youngest sister, Nina Boyd-Carpenter, and saw her sisters frequently, often seeking their opinion on important decisions. At a suitable age, the girls were sent to the Friends' School at Saffron Walden were they distinguished themselves academically, with the three eldest becoming head girl in turn. Alone of the four sisters, Margery then went on to Clark's College where her intelligence and application were recognised at once.

Before the outbreak of World War I it was unusual for a girl of Margery Fish's class to want, or to have the opportunity to follow, a career. It shows that she had a streak of independence that marked her out from most of her peers even at an early age. Her father was, by all accounts, a stern man and it seems likely that she had to battle with him to go to secretarial college, an experience that must have stood her in good stead when later she worked for men of strong will and dominating character. There is no evidence that it was her intention to follow her spell at Clark's with a career in Fleet Street but this is what happened.

3

No doubt her aptitude with words and her interest in the world at large led her to be drawn in that direction. It is likely that her parents did not approve of her decision but she had sufficient confidence to ignore their prejudice; an early manifestation of her willingness to go against the established order that later was such a feature of her approach to gardening. It comes as no surprise to find in the introduction to *We Made A Garden* these words: 'However imperfect the result, there is a certain satisfaction in making a garden that is like no one else's, and in knowing that you yourself are responsible for every stone and every flower in the place.'

She began her working life in Fleet Street in September 1912 as a secretary to the Advertisement Manager on the *Daily Mail* after a brief spell as a secretary to the Editor of the Country Gentleman's Publishing Company. Fleet Street must have been a revelation to a girl of Margery's sheltered upbringing but there is little doubt that she took to it immediately, or that her talents were recognised when, within a short time, she was promoted from the advertisement office to that of the paper's editor, Tommy Marlowe. Here, for the first time, she found herself working for Lord Northcliffe, the paper's founder. Northcliffe had edited the paper himself until the commitments of his expanding empire forced him to hand over to Marlowe, but he still kept in very close touch with his editor. 'The Chief', as Northcliffe was known to his staff, was a dictator who ruled his staff through a combination of fear and friendliness, arousing conflicting feelings of love and hatred in those he employed. It was said of him that he was 'swift to reward and equally swift to punish.' If Margery's father had been the dominating person in her early life, then Northcliffe was the man who exerted the greatest influence on her for the next ten years.

Alfred Harmsworth (later the first Viscount Northcliffe) had founded the *Daily Mail* in 1896; undoubtedly, he was a megalomaniac but he had a genius for gauging what the average person wanted to read. As a journalistic innovator he was unrivalled and the *Mail* heralded a revolution in modern journalism with its unique combination of news, gossip and photographs in an attractive format. Northcliffe was the first newspaper owner to anticipate the important contribution women would make to society as the 20th century unfolded, and the *Mail* became the

4

first daily newspaper to cater especially for women. In a world where women still had not been given the vote, it must have been exhilarating for Margery to work for an employer who was prepared to promote talented and hard working employees regardless of their sex. Working for him was as taxing as it was stimulating, requiring all Margery's intelligence and sense of humour – but she loved it. It is well known that he could behave like an overgrown schoolboy, full of kindness and generosity one minute and vehemently berating everyone within reach the next, but Margery always remained loyal to his memory. Northcliffe instilled in her the importance of aiming for the highest standards at whatever she embarked upon and through her work for his outstanding editor, Tommy Marlowe, she acquired the skill of simple, uncluttered writing. As a young man, Northcliffe had set up a weekly paper called *Answers to Correspondents*, whose keywords were 'interesting, extraordinary and amusing' – journalistic qualities he expected to find in his papers and which Margery might well have had in mind when she wrote her first article for *Punch*, 'Gardening with Walter', later extended to form the basis of her first book *We Made a Garden*.

As the leading newspaper owner at the start of World War I, Northcliffe was in a pivotal position in Fleet Street and was arrogant enough to believe that he wielded great power with the Government. He had acquired *The Times* in 1908 and was in constant touch with all the influential figures of the age and it was said that he worked like ten men. It must have been an exciting, but, at times, a daunting working life for a young girl still in her twenties but Margery excelled at it. When in 1917, Northcliffe was asked by the Prime Minister, Lloyd George, to head the British Mission to the USA, he requested that she be on his staff. She accepted without hesitation, dismissing the danger to the convoy from enemy torpedoes as it crossed and recrossed the Atlantic. It appears that she greatly enjoyed her stay in the USA, working hard and meeting her American relations, the Buttfields, for the first time. The relationship prospered and later, the family introduced Margery to one of her most famous gardening protégés, Lanning Roper. It was the first of several visits she made to North America and the beginning of a great love she had for the country, its people and its plants. The mission spent three years in the USA with Margery's contribution being recognised when she was awarded the MBE after the War. Northcliffe's regard for her is obvious in a letter dated 1921:

Letter from Lord Northcliffe, *The Times* dated 30th May 1921

My dear Miss Townshend,
I am sorry to hear that you are unhappy in Liverpool. I have been there for nearly a week and had I known you were there, I would have seen you. It is difficult to find appointments just now, but yours is an exceptional case. You crossed the Atlantic when the submarines were at their worst and I have always given special treatment to those of my staff who took the risk. I will do my utmost. Meanwhile please come and see me tomorrow, Tuesday morning at 11.30 at No.1 Carlton Gardens.
Yours sincerely,
Northcliffe

It seems likely that through Northcliffe's influence, Margery went on to become a Personal Assistant to Walter Fish who had been news editor on the *Daily Mail* and was later to become its editor. If Northcliffe was the innovator of the popular daily newspaper, then Walter Fish was responsible in large part for its development. He rose through the ranks of the journalistic world, finally becoming editor of the *Daily Mail* in 1922. Working for him must have been as exhausting as it was for Northcliffe and Tommy Marlowe, because he was exacting and quirky, but Margery had had years to prepare herself for it. Like his predecessor, Marlowe, Walter Fish was a dedicated journalist who impressed Margery with his combination of decisiveness and an unrestrained zest for life. As an editor, he could be a tyrant, but nevertheless she greatly enjoyed working for him, witnessed by her offer to carry on his secretarial work after he retired as editor in 1929:

Letter from Walter Fish to Margery dated 7th January 1930

My dear Miss Townshend,
I was more pleased than I can say to receive your letter. It has always been a very great pleasure to work with you and I shall miss our happy association very much indeed. But I am looking forward to seeing you frequently as I shall come to the office

fairly often. It is very nice of you to offer to help me with my correspondence, but that does not surprise me as I have always found you the most willing girl in the world.
Ever yours sincerely,
Walter Fish

Margery had worked for Walter Fish for about seven years when this letter was written and it shows clearly that their relationship had been entirely professional. However by the end of March of the same year, Margery had received a much more personal letter from Walter in which he said, 'Although we have seen each other for years, it is strange how little time we have ever had to talk. That is why it was so jolly to be able to talk to you the other evening apart from business concerns.' Two years later, on March 2nd 1933, they were married; Margery was forty one and Walter was fifty eight. The caption below the photograph that appeared in the papers at the time described Margery as 'one of the most charming and efficient women in Fleet Street.' Her first career had ended but within a few years she would embark on her second and more illustrious one.

After their marriage, Walter and Margery continued to live in London, first in Chilton Court near Baker Street and later in Vicarage Court, Kensington. Walter remained on the Board of Associated Newspapers and they led a busy and varied social life. Margery was always gregarious and loved entertaining and they were regular theatre and party goers. Henry Boyd-Carpenter, Mrs Fish's nephew, says of her that 'she loved the company of the great and the good', a desire for intellectual companionship that remained undiminished with age. She had always enjoyed music, particularly opera, and now she had the time and opportunity to indulge her interest. While she and her husband were living in town, two of her sisters had developed a love of gardening and tried unsuccessfully to interest their sister in it. When, years later, Mrs Fish had had several books published and was recognised as an eminent gardener, her sisters took great delight in reminding her of her former indifference. Before she and Walter left London, if given the choice between gardening and golf, she would certainly have chosen golf.

In 1937, with the threat of war hanging over Europe, the Fishes decided that they should find a country retreat while keeping their flat in Vicarage Court. To be within easy reach of town and in a mild climate, they started to search west Dorset, east Devonshire and Somerset. They first came to East Lambrook on a fine day in September of that year. The village, just north of South Petherton, is tucked away down narrow, winding lanes in an area of Somerset that had become prosperous originally through the wool trade. Later, this part of the Somerset Levels became a centre for cottage industries like basket-making, thatching and glove-making. The hamstone house that the Fishes had come to see dates from the 15th century, is long and low and set out in an L-shape, typical of Somerset houses of that period. Its history is uncertain but it is known that, at different times, it had been two cottages, a bakery, a post office, a farm and possibly a slaughter house. The south front with its small paved garden faces on to the village street, while the main garden, on the north side of the house, is sheltered from the road by a stone wall. A glimpse of the variegated sycamore through an open door into the rear garden delighted Mrs Fish; it was as if its fluttering sunlit leaves were a welcoming banner. However, the Fishes hardly had time to admire its merits on this first visit. The house was in a sad state; the tiled roof was patched with corrugated iron, the front garden was a jungle of rusty laurels and an overpowering smell of creosote did nothing to disguise the dank smell of an unlived-in house. Walter would venture no further than the hall. His reaction was quick and decisive; 'Full of dry rot. Not at any price.' With that, they turned their backs on East Lambrook and spent the next two months looking for a more prepossessing dwelling elsewhere.

In November, returning from a house-hunting excursion, they came upon a sign to East Lambrook. Curious to see what had happened to the house in the intervening months, they made a detour. There had been an amazing transformation. The offending corrugated iron had been replaced by old tiles, an attempt had been made to clear the front garden and the dank atmosphere had vanished, replaced by the fresh smell of new paint on woodwork and walls. This time Margery coaxed Walter beyond the threshold and they explored the house properly. They were enchanted with its stone and elm floors, the enormous stone fireplaces, beams, panelling and mullioned windows. Displaying their characteristic decisiveness, the Fishes decided there and then

8

that this should be their home after all. The Old Manor, as it was then called, became theirs for £1000. They had found their home by chance but afterwards Margery was glad that it happened to be in Somerset. 'Somerset is my county by adoption, but if I had to choose again I would not wish to change ... I have been grateful that the house we liked happened to be in Somerset.' She discovered the subtle beauty of the landscape and described it later to her readers in an article for *Homes & Gardens* magazine in 1962; 'On the whole I would not call it a spectacular county, although it is very varied. It has its grand moments in the rugged cliffs of Cheddar Gorge, it is ringed with hills to the east, south and west, and it possesses the lonely grandeur of Exmoor, with its little streams and frowning heights. But Somerset to me is the smiling countryside where I live, a countryside that has changed little through the years: green fields and apple orchards and streams lined with willows. Willows are everywhere: their fluttering leaves are cool in summer and in winter the shoots from the pollarded heads take on a tinge of red. Corot could have painted his pictures here, for the whole scene is one of tender loveliness, with softly luminous skies against blue mists in the distance.'

Having found their perfect house, the Fishes then had to hand it over to architects and builders. The next year was spent making it habitable while they hurried back and forth from London to oversee the work. Paint was stripped from paintwork and panelling, mullioned windows were restored and structural alterations were made. Finally the house was furnished hurriedly from London salerooms; furniture which Mrs Fish changed over the years as she found pieces better suited to the nature and period of the house. She had an instinctive flair for decorating, treating the interior of the house with as much sympathy and style as she later did the garden. She had an eye for harmonious use of colour: 'Colours in an old house have to be soft and mellow, no bright blues or hard dark greens, and reds should be faded to the colour of old brick. The only green I use is as light and silvery as the moss that grows under the beech trees.' In accordance with these principles, the cream distempered walls were eventually changed to a subtle shade of grey, green and ivory. Also, she loved the 'lived-in' character of faded fabrics and the patina of old country furniture. Valerie Finnis, the distinguished gardener, who stayed frequently at East Lambrook in the 1960s, was spellbound by the powerful atmosphere of the house. She remembers lying awake on warm summer nights, with the moonlight coming through the leaded windows, listening to the ticking of the grandfather clock and not daring to move in case the creaking boards disturbed the household. However, she admired the sympathetic way Mrs Fish had restored the house and how it seemed to have a casual, timeless look, like that of the garden: 'She had marvellous taste – there were faded fabrics, perfect furniture, parchment lampshades and modern hand-made silver tableware. Even in winter, there were always flowers in a container of moss on the hall table.'

It seems likely that her ideas on decorating and furnishing came from her innate aesthetic sense, rather than the restlessly varied decorative edicts of the time. However, there was a small, but influential group of people who were dedicated to the conservation and sympathetic restoration of old country houses in a way that made them suitable for contemporary living. Moreover, they insisted that the restoration of their houses went hand-in-hand with a suitable approach to the garden. Devotees of this country house cult included Colonel and Mrs Lindsay of Sutton Courtenay in Berkshire, Colonel Cooper of Cold Ashton, Gloucestershire and, of course, Vita Sackville-West and Harold Nicolson of Sissinghurst, Kent. All of them created gardens around their homes as part of a single vision, just as Margery Fish was to do at East Lambrook.

2

Margery Fish and Cottage Gardening

THE FISHES DECIDED that before tackling the garden, they must allow themselves time to get to know their home and establish themselves in their new surroundings. They realised that it would have to be the sort of garden they could tend themselves because they were still spending time in London and could garden only occasionally. There was also a conscious decision that the garden should be a personal domain; a place where they would be in control and where the physical work would not be left to the whim of a professional gardener. Furthermore, as Mrs Fish wrote, 'It is pleasant to know each one of your plants intimately because you have chosen and planted every one of them.'

The Fishes' garden – it hardly merited the name when they took it on – consisted of small areas of grass divided by stone walls and separated from the outbuildings by another wall. There were very few plants; the variegated sycamore (*Acer pseudoplatanus* 'Leopoldii'), a mass of 'Dorothy Perkins' roses, three *Fuchsia magellanica*, white arabis in the walls and Madonna lilies below them. In the area at the front of the house there was a jungle of rusty laurels, soapwort (*Saponaria officinalis*), a *Mahonia aquifolium*, an unidentified pink cabbage rose and the rose 'Great Maiden's Blush'. But Mrs Fish saw the limited content and lack of structure as an advantage: 'We were lucky that there was no garden around the wreck of a house. With a ready-made garden, even if it is neglected, there is always the temptation to leave some of the old features and work up to them instead of starting with nothing and creating a garden according to one's own ideas.' Although she had no gardening experience, it is clear that Mrs Fish was undaunted by the prospect of starting from scratch and, as with the house, she was determined that what she created should be suitable, practical and pleasing to the eye. The intention was that the new garden should be 'as modest and unpretentious as the house, a cottage garden in fact, with crooked paths and unexpected corners.'

Even in her early days at East Lambrook, Mrs Fish took time to look at other gardens in the area and at those of her friends and acquaintances. She would have seen examples of all the principal types of garden of the period. There was certainly diversity in gardening taste and some garden writers of the time were more than a little despondent about the state of gardening and the way it was likely to develop. Richardson Wright, then editor of *House and Garden* expressed the consensus view in *The Story of Gardening* published in 1934: 'It is rather difficult to choose from the whirlpool of contemporary gardening tastes and endeavours those that seem endowed with sufficient capacity for development to influence the course of future gardening.'

At this time the grander, labour-intensive gardens, often forming part of country estates, were in a state of decline. Their zenith, the so-called 'golden age of the British flower garden' had been in the Edwardian era when there was still a sense of security among the landed classes; 'Men still designed and planted in the belief that their sons and sons' sons would continue to enjoy the fruits of their labours and live on in conditions of progress and of peace', as Dorothea Eastwood wrote in 1958 in *The Story of our Gardening*. World War I marked the end of this creative period; optimism was shattered and the labour shortage, with consequential escalating labour costs, resulted in physical and financial burdens that could not be borne by many landowners. Others managed to keep their estates running at the expense of the garden. Fortunately, an awareness that the great estates could no longer survive unaided brought about the introduction of the Country House Scheme in 1937. Subsequently, under the auspices of the National Trust, the owners and their heirs could continue to live in the country home while the burden of maintenance of house and garden was removed from their shoulders.

Although Mrs Fish may have visited such grand gardens, she was much more familiar with the sort of garden that was preferred by the prosperous middle class to which she belonged. While the inter-war years marked a decline in the fortunes of the upper classes, the middle classes expanded and increased in affluence. There was money to spend on luxuries and they could choose to live in town or country. This resulted in the large suburban garden and the small country garden resembling one another in form and content. These gardens could have afforded their owners the scope to demonstrate their individuality, but most were unimaginative and what went into them had little to do with the art of gardening and much to do with demonstrating the owner's social and financial status. The characteristic ingredients were an abundance of bedding-out plants and a formal rose garden set in a sunken paved surround, often containing Hybrid Tea varieties rising from neat, bare earth. There would have been the obligatory herbaceous border – double if room allowed – and it would have been backed by a small group of flowering trees, including examples of the showy Japanese cherries which had recently been introduced and which were much sought after. The advent of better lawn seed, weedkillers and elaborate machinery allowed lawn space to be extended and in the larger gardens a tennis court/croquet lawn was a prerequisite. There may have been space for a shrubbery, a garden house and an ornamental pond, generally surrounded by crazy paving and fussy planting. Both house and garden were labour intensive and at least one professional gardener was employed and in the larger gardens they numbered, on average, one per acre. The owners seldom gardened themselves; to them the garden was a decorative extension of the house and a social playground, to be admired from a safe distance: 'Going around the Garden' was a popular lampoon of the time.

Mrs Fish's wish to create and maintain the garden herself placed her ahead of her time, as practical gardening for the upper middle class was still largely a thing of the future. Although, in general, middle class gardens were somewhat unimaginative at this time, it is likely that Mrs Fish would certainly have noticed those of a more individual character. *Country Life* often featured those with a certain extravagant elegance that harked back to Edwardian opulence. This was most apparent in the frequent use of richly draped pergolas, one-colour borders and massed herbaceous planting in the Gertrude Jekyll manner.

There were also a few exceptional gardens being created during this period, whose quality set them far above the standard. Each in its own way demonstrated its creator's originality of design and skill as a gardener. One that epitomised this individuality was the Savill Garden in Windsor Great Park that was begun in 1932 by Colonel Eric Savill (later Sir Eric), then the Deputy Ranger of the Park. He was a knowledgeable plantsman and a perceptive gardener, who understood how and where to grow plants to give them suitable habitats and show them off to best effect. Bulbs were naturalised in grass, primulas, primroses and meconopsis flourished in the moist and shaded areas, and his collections of unusual and tender plants were cosseted in sheltered beds. Mrs Fish came to know this garden well in later years and described it as the perfect woodland and water garden.

Vita Sackville-West and Harold Nicolson also admired the Savill Garden and adapted some of Colonel Savill's ideas at Sissinghurst Castle in Kent, where they created their unique garden. Here Harold Nicolson's framework of classical formality composed of linked enclosures formed of clipped yew and ancient brick, paved paths and stately vistas, provided the setting for Vita Sackville-West's flowering cornucopia. Her admiration for William Robinson's gardening ideals and her association with the country house cult gardeners provided the background for Sissinghurst's success, but it was her own inspired planting that turned success into supreme artistry. Tintinhull in Somerset was another exemplary garden of the time in a similar tradition. Here Mrs Phyllis Reiss, from 1925 onwards, remodelled and enlarged the existing garden with a sensitive touch. The garden was set out on different levels in a series of rooms which accorded perfectly with the simple elegance of the house's Queen Anne façade. Mrs Reiss used modern ideas of ground cover, with an emphasis on texture and foliage form, mixed shrub and herbaceous planting and created limited colour borders and areas planted for seasonal interest, in a way that simplified without loss of variety. Dame Sylvia Crowe wrote of Tintinhull in her book *Garden Design*: 'Its planting is probably unique because it combines a use of very varied species grown naturally, and yet strictly as elements of design.' In fact Mrs Reiss, together with Mrs Clive of Brympton d'Evercy nearby, was to become one of Mrs Fish's early gardening mentors and plant-hunting companions.

Another notable amateur gardener of the period was Mrs Norah Lindsay, whose own garden at Sutton Courtenay in Oxfordshire was a charming blend of ideas from many sources. In particular, she drew inspiration from the gardens of Renaissance Italy and the English cottage garden with its topiary and containing hedges, overlaying everything with her own exuberant style that was far removed from the carefully ordered colour swathes of Miss Jekyll and her followers. Mrs Lindsay believed in free-hand planting; her plants rose and fell in flowing peaks, fronds, spires and spikes, while self-seeded guests found a welcome home among more noble inhabitants. In his book *The Education of a Gardener*, Russell Page describes her talent: 'She lifted her herbaceous planting into a poetic category and gave it an air of rapture and spontaneity.' She designed parts of other gardens, for example, the simplified formal garden at Blickling Hall, Norfolk, in 1930, and a small knot garden at Mottisfont Abbey in 1938, but is best known for her influence on the development of Hidcote and her long friendship with its creator, Lawrence Johnston. Later, Mrs Fish became friendly with Mrs Lindsay's daughter Nancy, also a keen and imaginative gardener, whom she considered planted with a greater degree of skill than anyone else. Mrs Fish's gardening style, at least in part, bore similarities to that of both Mrs Lindsay and Nancy.

But for all the ideas and sights that may have fuelled Mrs Fish's imagination over the years, it was undoubtedly within East Lambrook and the surrounding countryside that much of her gardening philosophy was formed. The cottage gardens of the area with their unassuming and happy natures produced an immediate and lasting response in her that sparked off a desire to learn more about them. To understand the way Mrs Fish's garden developed, the history of the cottage garden deserves a fuller discussion.

Flowers have been man's companions throughout history, but the cottage gardener and his peasant antecedents always valued them highly, not only for their beauty, but also for their practical uses and their spiritual associations. They helped him cure sickness, gave him colour, scent and flavour and were his tribute on occasions of birth, marriage and death. More than that, they showed him the wonder of nature. From its humble beginnings to the picturesque idyll we associate with the term, the cottage garden has had a long and erratic development; it was shaped by the area of the country in which it lay, the merits of the local landlord, the enterprise of the cottager and the social history of the area.

In the origins of the cottage garden it is difficult to separate fact from legend. By the late Middle Ages, peasants were increasingly demanding wages for their labour and were able to rent land from the lord of the manor. For the first time, they had rights and were able to build cottages on their ground and plant crops of vegetables for the household. Here, in what were the first cottage gardens, they grew onions, garlic, leeks, cabbages and kale. It seems likely that parsley and fennel were grown too, as were wild strawberries, gooseberries and cherries. For the less fortunate, the 'garden' was probably no more than an enclosed yard to keep a pig, a strip of grass for sheep grazing and a row of corn, cabbages and beans to supplement a basic meat diet.

It is probable that the monastic gardens were responsible for the evolution of the cottager's vegetable patch into a garden with flowering plants and herbs. Manuscripts dating from the 9th century show monks cultivating patches of ground; they grew medicinal herbs for treating the populace in the monastery's infirmary, but also vegetables, salads and fruit crops for their own use. As the religious houses played such an important part in the life of that time, the monks' gardening skills must have been copied by the cottager. He would then have started to grow some of the monks' plants himself, many of which were gathered from hedgerow and woodland. Among these were clove scented pinks, *Dianthus caryophyllus*, cowslips and primroses – used to flavour drinks and wine – and violets, the flowers of which were added to salads. There would also have been some plants that, it is believed, were brought to Britain by the returning Crusaders – *Lychnis chalcedonica*, *Lilium martagon*, *L. candidum* and *Rosa gallica*. Herb Robert, wild scabious, mullein, mallow, columbine and St John's wort were grown for their medicinal properties as well as for distilling and drying, when they emit a sweet fragrance. Meadowsweet, southernwood and wormwood earned their place in the cottage garden because they were used for strewing on floors and to keep away fleas. Hyssop, lavender, sage and rue were also commonly grown for their scent and medicinal uses, as were fennel and coriander, valuable for their scented seeds. Plants such as dandelion, sorrel, scabious and tansy were distilled and made into toilet water. Nothing was grown that did not have a use, but by virtue of the plants' flowering nature, the cottage domain started to develop into a flower garden. Gradually, as more and more plants found their way into it, every space was filled and as its conditions imitated those of the plants' natural habitat, they thrived – close association suited them. No doubt the cottager took good care of his garden; it was essential for health and improving the conditions of life, but moreover it was one of his few personal possessions.

The Dissolution of the Monasteries after 1530 resulted in the loss of hundreds of monastic gardens. This meant that the cottager's collection became even more comprehensive as he could no longer look to the monastery for his medicinal needs. Prunella was grown for healing wounds and winter savory to ease the pain of wasp stings. Primitive sanitary conditions required skilled use of plants to cleanse the body and air. Toilet water was made from the distilled petals of the red rose and roots of *Rhodiola rosea* and women bathed their faces in the distilled leaves of woodruff. Many of the plants were used to make pot-pourri and great yellow loosestrife was dried and hung from the ceiling to keep away flies. Although the cottager primarily sought out useful plants, he also took home rarities that he came upon in the woods or hedgerows; plants like double primroses and unusual violets. In this way, his garden became a sanctuary for mutants that would have otherwise disappeared. There is little evidence about how the cottager arranged his garden in these early days. It is likely that there was no contrived lay-out, merely a busy profusion of herbs, flowers, vegetables and fruit.

By the early Elizabethan period, it was common for the cottager's smallholding to be as large as four acres. For the first time, flowers were grown purely for decoration, with vegetables and fruit grown separately, perhaps behind a screen of larkspur and cornflowers. Gradually the garden became the woman's domain, and took on a more orderly appearance. Many cottagers adopted a simplified version of the Tudor knotted bed, where low hedges of dwarf box, cotton lavender, thrift and marjoram were laid out in intricate patterns containing small beds of pinks, primroses, violets and double daisies. The cottager also started to clip his hedges into simple topiary shapes – imitating the grand gardens of the landowners. By the mid 17th century, the oriental hyacinth, *Ranunculus asiaticus, Colchicum byzantinum* and star of Bethlehem (*Ornithogalum umbellatum*) had found a home in the cottage garden. From the 1560s onwards, the Huguenot artisans fleeing from persecution on the Continent, brought new species, among which were the auricula and erythronium. These émigrés were responsible for starting the cultivation of 'florists'' flowers in Britain – flowers that were bred solely for their beauty rather than for any practical use. As they need intensive cultivation but little space, they were convenient for growing in the cramped houses of the Huguenot weavers and lacemakers, many of whom settled in East Anglia and the North. At first, these specialist growers cultivated and improved an enormous range of flowers for show, but at the end of the 18th century, there were only eight accepted show species. They were the anemone, auricula, carnation, hyacinth, pink, polyanthus, ranunculus and tulip. After 1800, the list was extended to include the dahlia, pansy, chrysanthemum, fuchsia, sweet William, iris, cineraria, phlox, hollyhock, verbena, heath and pelargonium. By 1600 the hardier forms of these flowers had become members of the cottage garden flora and, although the artisans continued to dominate the shows, much of the culture and future conservation of these plants was carried on by the cottage gardener.

Every year new plants were finding their way into the cottage garden; among them *Ranunculus aconitifolius, Fritillaria meleagris, F. imperialis* and the tulip that was introduced towards the end of the 16th century. Although the cottager was ruled by common sense and necessity rather than fashion, he was always willing to accept and exchange ideas and knowledge. In this way, a relationship developed between him and the manor's gardener, whereby the professional offered his know-how and handed out cuttings and discarded plant material. For the educated, good advice was also given through the written word of Thomas Tusser's *Five Hundred Pointes of Good Husbandrie* of 1557 and William Turner's *Herball* of 1568. However, it is scarcely likely that the average cottager would, or could, have read them, although he may have learned something of their content from the manor's gardener. By 1629, when John Parkinson published *Paradisi in*

Sole Paradisus Terrestris, gardening was a major recreation of the English upper classes. Rural England flourished with better housing, improved farming methods and a little more leisure for the labourer to enjoy his garden. This is not to say that the countryman's life was idyllic; progress was erratic, depending on the vagaries of the weather and local social conditions. He may have enjoyed an abundant harvest and made a good living for his family one year, only to be reduced to near starvation the next.

Interestingly, before the Tradescants made their horticultural odysseys to the New World in the 17th Century, returning with all manner of discoveries, most flowers in the cottage garden were either blue, purple or yellow. The Tradescants were responsible for introducing many plants which became ingredients of the cottage garden: double daffodils, anemones, spiderwort (*Tradescantia virginiana*), the perennial aster, golden rod, helenium and rudbeckia – all hardy plants that added colour and variety to the cottage garden palette. Later, the dahlia came from Mexico and chrysanthemum from China and Japan, whose late colour extended the flowering season.

After the Restoration, many gardens of the nobility were converted to the formal French style and, by William and Mary's reign, the parterre had superseded the knot garden. Great emphasis was put on bedding plants, such as the hyacinth, tulip and narcissus. The cottage garden remained, as it always had, unmoved by fashion and preserved old cultivars and species of such plants as the sweet William, pink, double primrose, gold laced polyanthus, old ranunculus and shrub roses. Very often these were hardier, more graceful and more fragrant than the new hybridised varieties grown in the large gardens. There was no sentiment or aesthetic preference on the part of the cottager who saved what otherwise might have been lost forever; he simply did not have the money to buy the new and expensive plants.

The Enclosures Acts in the second half of the 18th century, allowed the development of landscape gardening on the grand scale which often meant the destruction of cottages, even whole villages, that did not fit into the idealised view. Sometimes new cottages were built in the picturesque style, sometimes the unfortunate inhabitants were simply turned out to seek a home elsewhere. Although the Enclosures Acts compensated the people by the provision of allotments, often this option was not taken up as the cottagers were not aware of their rights. When the plots were cultivated, they were used to grow wheat or barley, potatoes and a few old fashioned flowers. Of course, the destruction of the cottager's life in this way affected only a minority. Elsewhere, the cottager was once more responsible for conserving many plants lost from the large formal gardens when they were replaced by grandiose landscape schemes. Another reason for the change in some cottager's lifestyle was the introduction of factory technology. Many cottage industries were destroyed by the invention of the Spinning Jenny, Arkwright's spinning machine of 1769 and Watt's steam engine of 1775. With a growing industrial economy, countrymen moved into towns to find work, resulting in rising wheat prices with no increase in wages. Very often, the garden stood between the cottager and starvation.

During the 18th century, an interest developed among the upper classes in the cottager's lifestyle; a romantic rather than a realistic view. It was not until well into the 19th century that artists, poets and authors, particularly those of the Arts and Crafts Movement, attempted to make a more realistic evaluation of the countryman's way of life. They appreciated nature's serenity, the value of the cottage craftsman's art and the idea that beauty did not have to be on a grand scale. However, 'cottage life' became something of a cult, bringing with it a patronising attitude towards the genuine cottager. There was a great difference between cottage life considered as an art form and the reality of the cottagers' lives.

The painting of such artists as Birket Foster and Helen Allingham minutely illustrate typical cottage gardens of the time and show two classic layouts. In one, the house stood near the road and had a small front garden enclosed by a hedge. This area was devoted to flowers, with the larger back garden given over to vegetables and fruit. In the other, the cottage was set well back from the road and had a path leading to the door. The path was edged with flower beds which screened rows of vegetables. There were flower beds beneath the windows too, and a great variety of climbing plants grew on the house. Jasmine, convolvulus, passion flower, clematis or roses covered the walls and draped the porch. The list of plants grown was by now too extensive to give a full account but a typical sample would include pinks, sweet

Williams, hollyhocks, wallflowers, sweet briar (*Rosa eglanteria*), R. 'Great Maiden's Blush', mignonette, stocks, sweet peas and larkspur. Bedding plants included pelargoniums, dahlias and china asters and among the bulbs were tulips, crocuses, snowdrops and lilies.

It was not only artists who promoted interest in the countryside and its flora. In 1822, John Claudius Loudon published his *Encyclopaedia of Gardening*, followed in 1828 by the *Gardener's Magazine* and *The Manual of Cottage Gardening* in 1830. His greatest influence was on the growing number of urban 'cottage gardeners' to whom he addressed *The Suburban Gardener and Villa Companion* published in 1838. In 1848, G.V. Johnson started *The Cottage Garden Magazine* – in 1868 the title was changed to the grander *Horticultural Journal* – and William Robinson founded *The Garden* magazine in 1871. These publications were aimed at middle and upper class gardeners, but *Amateur Gardening* of 1884 was a success with both cottagers and suburbanites. For better or worse, it put the cottage gardener in touch with contemporary ideas and technology. This type of educational reading was quite new to him, as previously he had relied almost entirely on hand-me-down knowledge. At about the same time, the style of many cottage gardens changed as mixed hardy planting and carpet bedding were more used. It followed the inevitable pattern, that while the use of bedding plants declined in popularity in large gardens, it was adopted by the small ones. The cottage garden had become a miniature time capsule of styles taken on from the gardens of the gentry, but now it was the turn of the cottagers to shape the ideas of their grander neighbours.

By the end of the 19th century, artisans, civil servants, retired gentry and independent gentlewomen, were living alongside the farmers and cottagers. In this mixed village society gardening provided, and still does, a camaraderie where, irrespective of circumstances, knowledge was shared and seeds and cuttings exchanged over the garden fence. New plant introductions of this period included the large-flowered delphinium, more dahlia varieties, *Clematis × jackmanii*, Japanese anemones, hybrid irises and Hybrid Perpetual roses. Among the new shrubs were *Kerria japonica*, *Ribes sanguineum* and *Fatsia japonica*. These found their way into the cottage garden as cuttings from the manor or via that other invaluable source of plant material, the rectory.

In the Edwardian period, the cottage garden influence was evident in the herbaceous planting of many large gardens – a theme that William Robinson vigorously encouraged and which was continued by Gertrude Jekyll, who made cottage flowers the foundation of many of her planting schemes. The Edwardians also revived the artifice of enclosing their gardens into 'rooms' with hedges and walls, as exemplified by Lawrence Johnston's garden at Hidcote. Just how far the cottage garden had come from its humble origins was shown when Vita Sackville-West described Hidcote as 'a cottage garden on the most glorified scale.' Her own garden at Sissinghurst raised cottage gardening into an exquisite art.

During World War II, when so many of Britain's gardens were given over to the vital production of food, the cottagers and their allotments made their own contribution to the effort; the allotments produced a million and a quarter tons of produce per annum during the war years. After the war, the traditional cottage garden went into decline, partly because self-sufficiency was no longer a way of life and partly because of the influence of gardening magazines, television and radio. People moved home more often and were susceptible to the fashion for instant effect in their gardens.

When Mrs Fish started making her garden at East Lambrook, old cottage gardens still existed but many plants had already been lost or had become extremely rare. She could see that their traditions were being eroded as she noted sadly in 1961: 'I am afraid the cottages and their little gardens may disappear completely as the years go by and we shall have to remember them by the flowers.'

Influences on
Margery Fish

W HEN MARGERY FISH died she left her library of gardening
books to her nephew, Henry Boyd-Carpenter. He says she
was always conscious of being an amateur gardener and suffered
from feelings of inadequacy when dealing with some of her pro-
fessionally-trained colleagues. As her interest grew, and perhaps
to compensate for what she regarded as a shortcoming, she went
to evening classes in botany at Taunton and began collecting
botanical and horticultural books, referring to them frequently.
She learnt quickly; within a few years of starting to garden, she
was able to write knowledgeably, lucidly and with humour about
her newly-acquired interest. In her garden, when faced with
increasing numbers of visitors, she wore her expertise lightly but
was never at a loss for a plant name or its provenance. Interestingly, however, she disliked having to use Latin names when
faced with questions from the general public, believing that too
many of them could deter an aspiring gardener.

Although she was a voracious reader she gave no clues about
which books were the first to fire her enthusiasm. There is no
doubt that she was inspired by books but they never took
over her imagination completely; it was her instincts coupled
with her vast expertise that ultimately produced her distinctive
garden.

Among her books were those of William Robinson, although
there are almost no references to him in her writing. He, more
than any other garden writer, including even Gertrude Jekyll, is

responsible for the way English gardening has altered in the 20th century and his books, in particular *The Wild Garden* (1870) and *The English Flower Garden* (1883) were the core of Mrs Fish's library. Robinson, like Mrs Fish, loved plants passionately and his approach to gardening stemmed from this fact. When writing of his feelings on first seeing some wild herbaceous species, he gives an indication of how much plants meant to him: 'It is beyond the power of pen or pencil to picture the beauty of these plants.' Robinson started to write when he was in his twenties but it was only when *The Wild Garden* appeared when he was thirty-two that he became well-known. The ideas propounded in the book were simple and not even particularly original. Writing in *A History of British Gardening*, Miles Hadfield says 'Robinson's aim was to obliterate the Paxtonian era and to pick up the threads again that Loudon let fall when he died.' It was his contention that the best way to grow plants was in as near a wild setting as possible, giving them conditions comparable to those of their natural habitat. Also, that it was possible and preferable to mix, what he called exotics (i.e. plants not native to the British Isles) with naturally occurring British species, thereby producing a different and much more interesting effect. When Mrs Fish gardened, these were exactly the principles she followed. Interestingly, however, she thought that the idea of a totally wild garden was impossible; in her experience plants left wholly to their own devices usually died. She writes repeatedly of the need for selecting the natural site for a plant, for close planting, for letting plants spread into each other to form mosaics and for allowing seedlings the chance to spring up and add to the thick planting, covering the soil as in nature. At the beginning of her book *Carefree Gardening*, she demonstrates how much she is in accord with Robinsonian philosophy: 'Instead of trying to make our gardens as different as possible from nature we now strive for a natural effect and aim at producing in a garden what nature does outside, but with cultivated plants.'

This 'wild gardening' was considered revolutionary when *The Wild Garden* was published and there was much resistance to it from the horticultural establishment of the time. We are all so used to seeing drifts of flowers in grass, waterside plants informally arranged around pools, herbaceous perennials with trees and shrubs in mixed borders and the universal use of ground cover that it is easy to forget that these practices arose in the late Victorian period and are directly attributable to the influence of Robinson and his followers. His aim was to interest everyone in the beauty of individual plants and to show how much the gardener could learn from nature about their use. It was not a question of imitating nature but of understanding her rules. Following his example, Mrs Fish learnt to observe all her plants very closely and to use them to produce a natural or wild effect. It may have looked as though her garden had arisen by accident, but in reality she placed each new plant in a position that would provide the best growing conditions. However, such was her belief in allowing nature to take its course that if seedlings appeared, she allowed them to proliferate provided they did not overwhelm other precious specimens or spoil the overall appearance of a particular part of her garden. As she wrote: 'Some natural plantings come about by accident and are better than if we had taken endless trouble to achieve a carefree effect. Nature's planting is often better than ours. In my ditch garden a fine self-sown *Geranium psilostemon* appeared under a willow. I have always grown it in full sun but its magenta flowers are more intense in the shade.' This minute examination of every small happening in her garden was characteristic; her excellent memory ensured that each incident could be put to good use later on.

Robinson's reputation as the originator of the 'wild' garden is so firmly established, that it is sometimes overlooked that he was a discerning admirer of cottage gardens and their plants or that he wrote about them so lovingly and enthusiastically: '... it is rarely nowadays that a large garden shows anything like the charm of simplicity that many cottage gardens do.' His descriptions in *The English Flower Garden* must have struck a chord with Mrs Fish. Early on in the making of her garden at East Lambrook she discovered the charm and diversity of these gardens and, as Robinson had also noted, that they were the repositories of many unusual and interesting plants. She did not hesitate to introduce them into her own garden and, later, did her utmost to interest her readers in these neglected plants.

Robinson's love of cottage gardens was shared by his friend and admirer, Gertrude Jekyll. Miss Jekyll, another profound influence on 20th-century gardening, was convinced that gardening, at its best, could be an art form. She always acknowledged her debt to Robinson, 'for whose good help I can never be sufficiently grateful.' There is no doubt that her influence on the Fish style was considerable because, like Robinson, she never wavered in her love of simple flowers and in the traditional gardening practices she observed in the cottage gardens of her native Surrey. But, whereas references to Robinson are few in Mrs Fish's writing, those to Jekyll and her particular plants are numerous. Perhaps this is because Robinson's influence on Mrs Fish was an all embracing one; their philosophies of gardening were more or less identical, whereas Miss Jekyll's influence on Mrs Fish was at a more practical level. Certainly they would not have been in complete agreement about how a garden should be planned or what its overall look should be. Miss Jekyll would not have liked the almost total informality of Mrs Fish's garden.

Miss Jekyll put into practice many of William Robinson's ideas. She excelled in under-planting woodland and the periphery of water so that it appeared 'natural' in the Robinsonian manner and she always took the trouble to relate her plants to the conditions they would have enjoyed in the wild. But whereas Robinson brought to his gardening, and thence to his writing, a profound love of plants and a deep practical knowledge, Miss Jekyll, the accomplished artist, brought an aesthetic approach in which her principal aim was to use plants to paint living pictures. In her book *Colour Schemes for the Flower Garden* she outlines her philosophy: 'The duty we owe to our gardens is so to use the plants that they shall form beautiful pictures ... I am strongly of the opinion that the possession of a quantity of plants, however good the plants may be themselves and however ample their number, does not make a garden; it only makes a collection. Having got the plants, the great thing is to use them with careful selection and definite intention.' For many years Margery Fish took this to heart; she had large collections of the species she most admired (for example snowdrops, primroses, euphorbias and hellebores) but tried never to let her enthusiasm for them cloud her judgement about their placing or the overall effect of her planting. It was a very difficult balance to achieve because in her garden there were so many plants in a relatively small space. Indeed, towards the end of her life, there were some who felt that she had lost the battle to maintain the balance because she was reluctant to let anyone else weed the garden. The exuberance of her planting and the number and diversity of seedlings could not be adequately controlled and the garden lost some of its artistic precision.

Although Miss Jekyll was a great philosopher of garden aesthetics she was also an expert practical gardener with an uncanny instinct for a good plant. As a writer, she never describes a plant or method of gardening without having had first-hand experience of it. When Margery Fish started to write about gardening, she followed this example. Penelope Hobhouse in *Gertrude Jekyll on Gardening* says of Miss Jekyll: 'she liked to study a plant, relating it to its natural habitat, and then used it appropriately, placing it comfortably next to plants with similar environmental needs.' While this took great skill, especially when planning the enormous herbaceous borders for which she is remembered, her real talent lay in arranging her carefully-chosen plants to produce supremely satisfying combinations. While Mrs Fish did not have Miss Jekyll's disciplined art school training, nor copied slavishly her ideas about colour, the garden at East Lambrook bore the stamp of someone who had read and absorbed her ideas about plant relationships.

If Mrs Fish acquired her love of plants in natural settings from Robinson and a feel for using plants to create pictures from Miss Jekyll, then there is no doubt that her interest in and love of more unusual plants came from meeting and reading the books of E.A. Bowles. Her writing is peppered with references to plants first grown or re-discovered by him and she was always quick to ascribe a plant in her garden as having come from his garden at Myddelton House near Enfield in Middlesex, one of the gardens she loved to visit: 'Anyone who has visited the garden will remember the variegated crown imperial *Fritillaria imperialis*, growing under the trees, or the wide planting of the Florentine iris under trees beside the New River.' Of the forms of *Helleborus foetidus* she wrote: 'I noticed the slightly different form of *H. foetidus* the first time I visited the late Mr Bowles's garden at Enfield, long before I had read his books.' On a decorative rhubarb she noted: 'Mr Bowles's Red Rhubarb *Rheum palmatum* is exciting from the moment the bright cerise buds come through the soil.' She became entranced by all Bowles's plants, many of which he had collected from the wild, and in time built her own collections.

Mrs Fish admired Bowles because he was the quintessential

plantsman. Also, she must have recognised a kindred spirit; like him she was a profoundly reserved person who did not reveal her feelings easily. Plants offered them both opportunities to display their generous and warm-hearted natures and form very close and lasting friendships. It is clear that the admiration was reciprocated because, having met Mrs Fish, Mr Bowles was anxious to divide and give her his most treasured plants. He was confident she would look after them. Mrs Fish wrote of Bowles's 'unerring eye for a good plant', and described him as 'many years ahead of his time, for he appreciated the kind of plants that we are only now learning to enjoy.' Among his passions were grasses, snowdrops, pulmonarias and celandines. He was amassing a collection of euphorbias when most people were still only familiar with the wild spurge of hedgerows. Under his influence euphorbias later became one of· Mrs Fish's favourite plants. He also wrote discerningly about hardy geraniums at a time when they were not at all common in gardens and it took the efforts of a populariser like Mrs Fish to interest a much wider audience in them. In writing about them she often shares Bowles's ideas: 'There is a definite tendency to use more and more informal plants like the geraniums, which need no staking, and look well wherever they are needed. We are beginning to value foliage for its own sake and appreciate the plants that keep their attraction when they have finished flowering.' She visited Bowles's garden whenever she could; there was an annual pilgrimage to see the snowdrops. It is obvious that she learnt much about planting from him. In a series of notes on how other gardeners cope with shade, she wrote: 'His mixed plantings under trees could teach us all a great deal. He grew plants of different texture, colour and form together to make a harmonious whole throughout the year. *Geranium ibericum* with its hairy leaves is next to the dark shiny foliage of *Helleborus niger*, with *Dicentra spectabilis* behind, lovely when dangling pink hearts hang among glaucous leaves. Among these he grew the poisonous hemlock, *Conium maculatum*, with its beautifully cut glossy leaves.'

Bowles's direct and humorous writing had immediate appeal. He became well-known to the gardening public and they flocked to see his garden. When in turn, Mrs Fish began to write, she, like Bowles was able to convey the warmth of her personality to her readers and they responded equally enthusiastically. Letters poured in with requests for her special plants and advice about specific gardening problems.

Vita Sackville-West had many gardening tastes in common with E.A. Bowles and with Margery Fish. But, as well as her discerning judgement of plants, she saw fantasy, mystery and romance as essential ingredients of the two gardens she created during her life, first at Long Barn and later at Sissinghurst. Mrs Fish regarded her as the best and most influential woman gardener of her generation. As they got to know one and other, there were times when Mrs Fish was in awe of the older and more experienced gardener because of her ability both to garden and write so brilliantly. The reasons why the two women were drawn to gardening could not have been more different. Vita Sackville-West's secure and privileged upbringing at Knole, timeless and remote from everyday life, gave her an enchanted view of the world. This dream-like existence was shattered when she discovered that the house she loved so deeply would never be hers. Jane Brown in *Vita's Other World* believes that the loss of Knole was the spur for Vita to create at Sissinghurst another world into which she could escape, a substitute for Knole. Harold Nicolson wrote of Sissinghurst much later as 'a succession of privacies: the forecourt, the first arch, the main court, the tower arch, the lawn, the orchard. All a series of escapes from the world, giving the impression of a cumulative escape ...' For Mrs Fish, the desire to create a garden stemmed merely from wanting to provide a suitable setting for the house at East Lambrook. Although it was a distinctive world of its own she would not have thought of it as an escape from reality nor was it prompted by that intense feeling for place that fostered Vita Sackville-West's gardening. Why then did Mrs Fish so respect Miss Sackville-West and why was she so influenced by her? There were several reasons. First because, despite being an amateur, Miss Sackville-West had, with the help of her husband, Harold Nicolson, created one of the greatest gardens in England. From her own experience, Mrs Fish knew that to produce such a garden needed more than just an artistic sense or knowledge of plants. It required painstaking daily devotion over a long period, during which the gardener took the time and trouble to observe all her plants minutely, moving them when they appeared unhappy and constantly rearranging groupings so that the attributes of each could be enjoyed within an overall picture. Mrs Fish was a dedicated gardener and she admired others, like Miss Sackville-West, who were equally dedicated because they had the same intense devotion to plants as she did. Here was a fellow gardener who planted with the utmost care yet was not afraid to break the rules; someone, like her, who would not shun a plant merely because it was common or of humble origin. While Sissinghurst owed much to the cottage garden and to the teaching of Robinson and Jekyll, its planting was primarily dictated by Vita's whim and taste forged through her love and knowledge of literature, her upbringing at Knole and her travels as the wife of a diplomat. Mrs Fish's garden had little in common with the formal elegance of Sissinghurst and East Lambrook's large collection of plants meant that there was no room for drifts of flowers, carefully arranged one-colour gardens or emphatic statements, but each visit to Sissinghurst yielded some new idea about the placing of plants that Mrs Fish adopted. She recorded the effects of one such visit: 'after seeing the double purple meadow geranium *Geranium pratense* 'Plenum Violaceum' in the violet garden at Sissinghurst Castle, I feel I have not given my plants the position they deserve and now I have planted the double white and double blue as well as the double purple forms in shady parts of my terrace garden.' There were many things that she admired at Sissinghurst while recognising that she had insufficient space at East Lambrook to emulate them. She intensely admired the single-colour gardens at Sissinghurst: 'The beautiful silver and white garden at Sissinghurst is a delight, and there is nothing more beautiful than white and silver plants against sombre old walls, such as courtyards and priory gardens. A gold and silver border is another luxury for the over-gardened, and one could have great fun finding just the right plants for it, but for most of us white and silver and gold must be woven into the tapestry of just one garden.' As a gardening writer Miss Sackville-West had what Robin Lane Fox calls 'a simple, personal tone with literary allusions and an artful air of romance.' She had the ability to fuel the imagination of her readers so that they were tempted to try her suggestions and give their gardens 'an air of happy accident.' As a novice gardener soon after the war, Mrs Fish was not only inspired by Vita Sackville-West's articles in *The Observer* but also learnt many practical tips. Moreover, she found to her delight that here was a distinguished gardener/writer enjoying and planting many of the treasures she had begun to accumulate in her own garden. Articles extolling the virtues of 'Darling Daisies', 'Nostalgic Auriculas,' 'Wild Fritillaries' and many others convinced her that her gardening instincts were right and that she must continue to seek out and grow all those neglected cottage garden plants before they were lost forever.

When Margery Fish's *We Made a Garden* was published in 1956, Vita Sackville-West reviewed it in *The Observer*, and her praise was generous: 'Crammed with good advice. I defy any amateur gardener not to find pleasure, encouragement and profit from it.' To have received such a tribute from the best amateur gardener of the age gave Mrs Fish immense pleasure and marked her out as a new and increasingly influential plantswoman.

4

The Making of
Margery Fish's Garden

Although I took it as a matter of course that now we had a house in the country I should work in the garden, I had no idea then of the fanatic I was to become.

WHEN MRS FISH arrived at East Lambrook, a complete novice to gardening, she had to rely on her husband's experience. He had had a garden before at Sydenham Hill, Kent and, with his customary assertiveness, had no doubt that his ideas on how a garden should look were right. For him, the elements were perfect lawns, paths, hedges and walls with flower colour concentrated at the height of the season. He was undoubtedly a fair weather gardener. The idea of walking around in the depths of winter to enjoy the subtle differences between varieties of snowdrop or hellebore would never have appealed to him. Intuitively, Mrs Fish felt that his 'limited gardening' was not the right approach: 'When I started, my idea was to make as long a season as possible but I received no encouragement from my husband.' Risking his displeasure, she gradually introduced plants of her own choosing, but her desire for an all seasons garden was not realised until she started to widen the range of planting in about 1950. It was at this time that, having come to terms with the death of her husband two years earlier, she felt able to explore her own ideas fully, allowing the garden to become more completely a reflection of her own tastes.

Despite their disagreements about the content of the garden, Mrs Fish had to admit later that her husband had taught her some sound gardening practice: 'I learnt a great deal from Walter that first year of gardening. The first thing I learnt was that he knew a great deal more about the subject than I thought he did.' He believed firmly in the need for structure in a garden and she always acknowledged that his ideas on this were right; more than twenty years after they had started the garden, she wrote of the need for a background of neatly cut lawns, well-trimmed edges and hedges to what she referred to as 'jungle gardening' – as she called her own particular style. Certainly his ideas on improving the heavy clay soil and the need for feeding plants were sensible. He insisted that they make compost and cajoled her into using bonfire ash on the borders, long before she realised the value of potash, demanding that it be used before rain washed away its goodness. It was Walter who pointed out that her practice of making beds raised above the level of a path or lawn was artificial and unnecessary; he convinced her that level beds not only appear larger but look far nicer. She remade the borders but made the mistake of placing upright stones along the edges. Again, Walter stepped in and made her see that they were a distraction from the plants. Flat stones were substituted – in Walter's time they formed a neat edge between the borders and the lawn and paths, but after his death, Margery allowed her plants to billow out and creep over the stones. Another lesson he taught her was the importance of planting in bold groups; something she had room to do in the early days but not always with plants of her own choice. Walter was a dahlia, delphinium and lupin man and had no time for the less showy plants in which Margery was already becoming interested. When she became an expert plantswoman with an ever-increasing number of plants to find homes for, there was neither room nor inclination to achieve the same effect.

During their first few months at East Lambrook, the Fishes removed the rubbish that was strewn about the old farmyard (later called the barton) to the north of the house. At the same time, they cleared the small front garden and removed the stone wall that divided the main garden at the rear of the house into two rectangles, piling up the stone into large heaps for later use. Also, they dismantled the rockery that someone had attempted to make beneath the wall between the garden and the outbuildings. All the while they were planning the form the garden should take.

Mrs Fish's first planting was done as soon as they bought the house; a hedge of *Lonicera nitida* to hide the back door and kitchen. Soon afterwards she and Walter decided that the eastern boundary wall should receive her attention as it had ugly jagged top stones along its length. Here, between the stones she sowed seed of alyssum, valerian, aubrieta and arabis and a few easy rock plants to soften the wall's outline until a more attractive capping method could be found. Years later the descendants of these first plants thrived in the wall itself; a reward for her tenacity as she had stuffed them into every crack and crevice. They were her answer to the problem of how to liven up a dull blank wall in early spring when there was little interest elsewhere in the garden.

Any rubbish from the barton that could not be burned or buried was put under the two walls between the barton and the orchard, to the north of the main garden, to form the base for a new rock garden. Here again, flat stones were placed to form a generous edging between rock garden and drive. The space between them provided Mrs Fish with her first opportunity to plant a gift of 'Dresden China' daisies. In time, daisies became one of her favourite plants and she grew many different varieties. It was one kind of small plant that Walter liked as much as she did, insisting that she plant them everywhere, even around the ornamental trees that they had just planted. Generally Walter did not like the small things she had begun to cherish and certainly would not tolerate any plant that was badly planted or unhealthy. He would remove any that did not meet his high standards, laying them on the path 'like a row of dead rats', as Margery later wrote.

Unfortunately, as Mrs Fish admitted later, being new to gardening she laid the stones of her rockery with an outward tilt, so that much of the soil was washed away with the first heavy shower. 'The stones had to remain as they were for several months, a monument to my ignorance, but one happy day a cousin with a genius for gardening (Allan Buttfield) visited us and remade the gardens for me. From the house the effect was a luxurious display of rock plants growing out of the wall.'

Even in these early days there was evidence of her unorthodox use of plants when she refused to confine herself to the use of alpines in her rockery, interspersing them with a selection of other plants. Her taste was unsophisticated; she mixed *Daphne cneorum* with a 'Mrs Popple' fuchsia, winter heathers, *Ceratostigma plumbaginoides* and many annuals that rewarded her by being the best she ever grew; a success that convinced her that gardening was all too easy. The Fishes agreed that a large lawn was essential for the main garden: 'The bigger the lawn, the more spacious the garden was one of my late husband's maxims.' Walter liked uncluttered space in the house as well as the garden, with no unnecessary detail. The lawn was his domain and he levelled the ground and sowed the seed with Margery and a gardener's boy acting as labourers. Mrs Fish later regretted that they had not taken more trouble to lay proper drains and remove the top soil before levelling, because moss reappeared in the lawn each spring. As a perfectionist, she was always disappointed with this less than first class result.

It was about this time that she made her first attempt at building a dry stone wall. With so much stone piled up around the garden, the Fishes decided that it would be a good idea to have a low wall between the lawn and the drive. Here, as in the eastern boundary wall, Mrs Fish planted alpines: stonecrops, white arabis and *Campanula portenschlagiana* to start with; later the planting became more interesting when she added rock roses, helichrysums, lemon alyssum, lavenders, erigerons, cheiranthus, dwarf irises and *Campanula carpatica*. She so enjoyed building the wall that she was determined to repeat the exercise in other parts of the garden. Within a year of her first attempt, she went on to build the walls of the terrace garden – a much more arduous task. She loved to work with stone: 'I'm glad I live in a neighbourhood where stone is plentiful, because I should have to change a lot of my gardening ideas if I could not lay my hands on a piece of stone whenever I feel one is needed. And that is very often.' While clearing the roadside bank outside the east wall of the garden, the Fishes were delighted when they found a fine stone wall supporting the top end of the orchard. It had become completely covered with soil which Margery removed and used to improve the bank further along the road and to lighten the heavy clay soil of the garden. She then planted hundreds of white, pink and red valerian seedlings in the bank and wall. Sadly, within a few years those in the bank disappeared but the ones in the wall flourished and multiplied.

Following their idea that house and garden should blend into one another, the Fishes paved the area between the lawn and the door leading into the hall – the principal room of the house. They were pleased with the result because the flagstones inside merged with the paving outside and provided the all-important link between house and garden. This idea was extended to the small front garden. Here the Fishes experimented with crazy-paving but it was not a success as they used a cold blue stone and did not level the ground sufficiently. Walter insisted that the stones be relaid in concrete but the result was far too neat for Mrs Fish's taste and she was glad when the concrete started to break up; indeed she helped the process along with the use of a crowbar, leaving gaps for the precious small plants she was beginning to accumulate, including all the creeping thymes she could get. Later, in 1956, she described this area as 'One of the most labour saving things I have.' By this time she had, of course, added to the planting – there were now erodiums, dwarf irises, dianthus and small daisies, 'With all manner of creeping things to fill the crevices and oust the weeds.' In the narrow beds around the paving Mrs Fish recalled that it was difficult to decide what to plant. Hortensia hydrangeas seemed an obvious choice but she and Walter could never agree on the best colour for these – he liked blue and she pink: 'If we had planted them he would have wanted to change the colour artificially, just as he urged me to get my hair dyed when the grey hairs became noticeable. I hate artificially-coloured flowers as much as dyed hair.' The idea was abandoned in favour of a selection of herbaceous plants that were never very satisfactory, not only were the beds too narrow to accommodate enough plants, but the 'American Pillar' rose they had planted here always made colour harmonies difficult.

Walter had very fixed ideas on how the drive and paths should be made and maintained, claiming that 'there was nothing to beat a good gravel path ... so hard that nothing would spoil the surface and weeds would find no foothold.' He insisted that the preparation be very thorough. Gravel paths require much maintenance; not only systematic weed-killing but also regular and meticulous rolling. Immediately, Mrs Fish saw the drawbacks of such a labour-intensive practice. She realised that, with the exodus of young men from the country to join the forces in World War II, there would never be a return to the days of cheap and plentiful village labour. Her instincts told her that she, along with the vast majority of gardeners, would in the future have to garden in a much more labour-saving way. After Walter died she had a covering of bitumen laid on the drive and paved the paths.

The bareness of the walls of the house, its outbuildings and surrounding walls, depressed the Fishes when they arrived at East Lambrook so they set about covering them as quickly as possible. Walter acquired a gruesome collection of stuffed animal heads and horns which were mounted, much to the astonishment of his wife and neighbours, on the inside and outside of every available outbuilding. Meanwhile, Margery was dispatched to the local nursery to acquire ampelopsis, roses, pyracantha, cotoneaster and *Clematis × jackmanii*. Walter thought that no other clematis was worth growing and Margery was too inexperienced in those days to disagree with him. She watched fascinated as he trained them tendril by tendril to cover the walls and frame the front door. Adapting the cottager's custom of growing summer-flowering jasmine (*Jasminum officinale*) over their porches and privies, Margery decided to cover a small stone house, now called the summer house, in the main garden with this sweet-smelling plant: 'In my childhood every cottage had a little house down the garden and this was romantically smothered with the plant. I could not resist copying the idea when we bought our house.' The Fishes had always admired the contrast of deep red roses against the golden local stone and so planted the bright double-flowered rambler 'Paul's Scarlet Climber', 'American Pillar' and the Hybrid Tea 'Climbing General McArthur' on the front and sides of the house. They chose the softer colours of pale pink 'Climbing Madame Abel Chatenay' and the apricot 'Climbing Lady Hillingdon' to train around the dining-room windows. Other climbing roses bought at this time included 'Climbing Ophelia,' 'Climbing Caroline Testout' and 'Gloire de Dijon.' The one climbing rose that Mrs Fish would not have been without was 'Albertine': 'At no other time am I so prodigal with flowers in the house. Bowls of 'Albertine' appear in every room.' Soon after they started the garden, Mrs Fish's sister, Nina, gave her a *Ceanothus × veitchianus* for the front of the house; its effect was glorious, but this ceanothus is short-lived and it had to be replaced every few years.

These early plantings were not especially adventurous; it was only later that Mrs Fish began to use the walls as a 'canvas,' experimenting with all kinds of unusual and tender plants to add an extra dimension to the garden. In 1961 she wrote an article on 'Three Decker Planting', which demonstrated how much her knowledge had advanced and how adept she had become at using every available space: 'It is wasteful not to make the most of walls, particularly when wall space is limited, and very often one can grow three different plants above each other.' In this article she suggests seventy-eight different plants that she knew from her own experience would enhance any garden – in fact by that time in her own garden she grew hundreds. She talks about growing *Convolvulus cneorum* at the bottom of one of her south walls with the penstemon *P. isophyllus* and the rose 'Climbing Madame Butterfly' above it. On the same wall she also grew the silver *Senecio vira-vira* (syn. *S. leucostachys*) as a foundation plant and allowed the climbing *Senecio scandens* and variegated *Coronilla glauca* to invade it, with the pink and cream splashed leaves of *Actinidia kolomitka* above. For planting against a west wall she suggests eucryphias, *Choisya ternata*, *Buddleja* 'Lochinch' and a selection of clematis – the species *C. flammula* and the cultivars *C.* 'Henryi' and *C.* 'Perle d'Azur'. At East Lambrook she used the buddleja in a sheltered corner between the cowhouse and the malthouse with *Ceanothus* 'Burkwoodii' behind. For east-facing walls she experimented with variegated ivies where space was limited, and suggests using white-flowered *Rubus* Tridel in places where its long arching stems can be accommodated easily. She used *Akebia quinata* to accompany the rubus and fill the upper section of an east wall, with *Forsythia ovata*, *Clematis alpina*, *C. macropetala* 'Markham's Pink' and *C. macropetala* to fill the middle sections and the dwarf *Mahonia nervosa* below.

She goes on to describe how she had fastened cattle fencing to an east-facing wall to give it more height and used it to grow a selection of climbing roses with the semi-hardy climber *Cobaea scandens* to ramble through them. North facing walls presented no problem for her; one of her plantings mentioned in the article was of a morello cherry which was then used to support *Clematis chrysocoma*. Elsewhere the winter-flowering *Clematis cirrhosa balearica* was planted near the climbing rose 'Zéphirine Drouhin.' In characteristically practical fashion she goes on to give planting tips: 'A good way to give an extra fillip to plants about to flower is to drive a crowbar in a little way from the roots and put in some bone meal.'

The ground to the west of the house sloped upwards towards an old orchard: 'nothing but a wilderness, and looked the most uninspiring material for a garden.' Margery tackled it in the winter of 1938. The only criterion she had was that it must not be too formal. She made a series of terraces, supported by low stone walls, separated by paths, with a broader, winding path leading up through the terraces to the orchard. The orchard was left rough, with daffodils planted in the grass, but in time it was tidied up and surrounded by a low hedge of lonicera. For the terraces she 'envisaged the beds as a tapestry of mixed colours rather than a series of herbaceous borders', and so she made a rough sketch, trampled out the design in the thin snow, marked the outline and started work. Later, she admitted that it had been a foolhardy enterprise for a complete novice to undertake. Not only had she to build the dry stone walls herself, removing endless barrowloads of heavy clay subsoil (while carefully mounding up the good topsoil for future use), but also she had to plant up the beds extremely carefully as they could be seen from all sides – one of the hardest of all planting exercises. In retrospect Mrs Fish was quite sure she had been right to persevere. She later wrote: 'A garden that is made on different levels takes on a look of maturity far more quickly than a flat garden that has to rely for its effects on the planting.'

By the following spring most of the manual work was done and Margery had carefully chosen plants for it, but Walter was disparaging, referring to the new garden as 'the floral quarry'. To Margery's dismay, he decided that it needed a line of 'pole roses' along the main path and, although she felt that they ruined the proportions, there was nothing she could do. As 'Walter's wife', it would never have occurred to her to go against his wishes. Later she could not remember all the ones they chose, but they included 'Cupid', 'Chaplin's Pink', 'Climbing Lady Hillingdon', 'Gloire de Dijon' and 'Paul's Scarlet Climber'. To Margery's relief this arrangement lasted only briefly and Walter finally agreed to remove them in the summer of 1940. The roses were replaced by small cypresses (*Chamaecyparis lawsoniana* 'Fletcheri') which were clipped into neat cone-shapes. In time these became known to her family as 'Margery's Pudding Trees'. The effect that these small trees had on the overall picture made Mrs Fish realise the importance of evergreens.

When she started to plant up the terrace beds, Mrs Fish realised she had too much space and not enough plants, so she used as many spreaders and easy plants as possible that had a long season and needed no staking. She used plants like *Geranium endressii*, white iberis, pulmonarias, *Oxalis articulata* and nepeta. Gypsophila, aubrieta and *Dianthus gratianopolitanus* were planted to spill over the top of the walls and the crevices were crammed with white arabis, London pride, stonecrops and rock campanulas. Her first success with simple cottage garden plants encouraged her but she was aware of the importance of the careful choice of colours necessary for this sort of gardening: 'Very soon after I started gardening I was warned against using strong colours if I wanted to mix them ... In a cottage type of garden it is inevitable that colours intermingle.' Years afterwards, she thought that these early plantings had their virtues: 'Now that I have a hundred plants to every one I had then, I cannot indulge in such big patches of colour; taller plants have crept in, and the flowers are not so artlessly showy as in the early days.'

When the Fishes bought the property, part of its western boundary behind the malthouse was formed by a water-filled ditch. They bought a strip of the neighbouring orchard beyond the ditch with the intention of making a water garden. The bottom of the ditch was widened and flat stones were laid to make pools and waterfalls, but no sooner was this done than for no apparent reason the water disappeared. Margery was philosophical about this and realised the opportunities offered by a damp but accessible site. The pollarded willows growing in the ditch were kept as support for the banks that were cleared and made into a series of pockets, supported by large stones. At first the banks were planted with alpine strawberries, violets, London pride, primroses and primulas. Later on the ditch became the home of many treasures, including collections of snowdrops, rare primroses and polyanthus.

In the early 1950s a section of one of the banks was scooped out and filled with peat so that Mrs Fish could experiment with acid-loving plants, a long cherished wish: 'If you are one of those fortunate people with no lime in your soil, you may not realise how frustrating it is to be debarred from all the exciting things that will not tolerate lime.' This first attempt at making the bed proved disastrous and all the plants died, so her cousin, Allan Buttfield helped her remake it, and gave her a collection of heathers for its first planting. Later she tried dwarf rhodo-dendrons, azaleas, *Epigaea asiatica*, ramondas, haberleas and *Cornus canadensis* – 'A wonderful ground-cover for those lucky people who can let it ramp, as it works fast and covers itself with typical dogwood flowers, fat and white, gazing up to the sky.' As her knowledge broadened, she introduced a few orchids, including *Dactylorhiza elata*, and *D. foliosa*. She tried more unusual daphnes too – *Daphne collina*, *D. arbuscula* and the variegated *D. cneorum*.

Behind the malthouse the ditch turns at right-angles and here Walter worked hard to make a miniature cascade, but the water disappeared before he had finished it. Here Margery put plants that relished sun or moisture – on the shady side primulas, *Iris ensata*, and *Meconopsis betonicifolia* and in the sun, rock roses, sternbergias and androsace.

One of Mrs Fish's most attractive qualities – valuable to all gardeners – was her ability to laugh at herself and admit mistakes: 'In our endeavours to make the garden more interesting we made every mistake that was possible. Very early in the game we decided we must develop vistas in the garden to add interest and purpose. In a small garden it is difficult to achieve the unexpected. We wanted our garden to be "come hitherish".' One of their early failures was the making of 'the shrine'. In an effort to bring the orchard area into the garden, they laid a path through the fruit trees, ending in a small paved court. But they had neither time nor labour to control the weeds that quickly invaded, so the whole thing was dismantled. Another error was their choice of hedging material. They thought that one of their first jobs must be to screen the property from the road on the south side and their neighbours' on the west, so they planted a hedge of *Cupressus macrocarpa* which after thirteen years died, as they were warned it would. It was replaced with *Lonicera nitida* which proved to be too flimsy for a tall hedge and so, in 1959, Mrs Fish had a wall built. She noted that it would not make such a good background as evergreen trees but was excited by the thought of having 130 feet of wall to cover with plants. As the cultivated area expanded, without, as Mrs Fish admitted, any overall plan, they realised the need for structure to define the different parts of the garden.

Again, *Lonicera nitida* was used to make enclosing hedges between the top terrace and the small orchard; around the vegetable patch (now the silver garden) and behind the malthouse to hide the compost heaps. In retrospect Mrs Fish regretted using lonicera for these low hedges because it grew so fast and needed trimming three or four times a year.

From her earliest days at East Lambrook, Mrs Fish found that the local people were always willing to part with plants if she showed an interest in them: 'I feel very humble when I think of the plants that are given to me so generously from the smallest gardens.' Before the war a baker's roundsman gave her *Bergenia* × *schmidtii*: it was her introduction to bergenias, for which she was very grateful. Not all her gifts proved to be so welcome. *Centaurea montana* from a neglected rectory garden became something of a menace as Mrs Fish discovered. During the war a local farmer was persuaded to accept a precious half pound of tea in exchange for a double primrose which she called *Primula × juliana* 'Jill'. Other early finds in the village included *Leucanthemella serotina* (syn. *Chrysanthemum uliginosum*) and *Corydalis solida*, at the time a connoisseur's plant. In later years Mrs Fish, who was renowned for her generosity, would, like the villagers, divide any of her plants and give them to anyone who showed a genuine interest in them: 'One of the most delightful things about gardening is the free-masonry it gives with other gardeners.'

Once she started to acquire plants for her garden, Mrs Fish became an avid reader of nursery catalogues and a regular customer of her local nursery Scotts of Merriott. Today, we are so used to having access to pot-grown plants that it is easy to forget that at the time Mrs Fish was gardening most plants started life in nursery beds. She realised the importance of buying her plants from a source with similar soil pH when possible. Her own soil was heavy clay with a pH of 8. When new plants were delivered, tending to them took priority over everything – including guests waiting for lunch. Not only was she fortunate in having a distinguished nursery on her doorstep but also numerous interesting gardens in this part of Somerset from which she could learn a great deal, notably Montacute, Tintinhull, Brympton d'Evercy and Barrington Court, the borders of which had been planned by Gertrude Jekyll.

It was during these early days that she met two gardeners who were to exert an enormous influence over her; Mrs Violet Clive of Brympton d'Evercy and Mrs Phyllis Reiss of Tintinhull. Both had fascinating and well-established gardens that intrigued the new gardener. They went out of their way to share their passion for plants with her and to encourage her. The spell cast by their houses and gardens never faded. Many years later, in the late 1960s, Mrs Fish was still writing of Brympton as 'the most beautiful house I have ever seen' and of Tintinhull's 'blessed feeling of serenity.'

Mrs Clive was the elder of the two women. She was born in 1875 and developed into a highly accomplished but eccentric personality. Her fierce independence showed itself, not only in her life, but also in her garden. Although she read widely, she never revealed the source of her gardening knowledge or whose style she admired. Undoubtedly she must have been influenced by Miss Jekyll in the way she 'softened' the rather formal Victorian planting of Brympton. People who remember the garden in her time compared it to the planting at Sissinghurst, but she was gardening in this style just after World War I – long before Vita Sackville-West went to Sissinghurst. She loved simple cottage garden plants and encouraged Mrs Fish to look closely at the cottage gardens in East Lambrook and the neighbourhood and to visit other notable gardens in the area. As their friendship developed they would often go out plant-hunting together in Mrs Clive's chauffeur-driven car, stopping outside cottage gardens that might have interesting plants, in the hope that the owner could be persuaded to part with bits of them.

Mrs Clive's absorption with the minute details of plants – the beauty of individual form and foliage – and a feeling for placing plants impressed Mrs Fish. Also, her ability to use foliage as a foil for architectural features and complement the hamstone of Brympton was a skill which Mrs Fish learned to apply at East Lambrook.

Captain and Mrs Reiss of Tintinhull first got to know the Fishes in 1940. Mrs Reiss could not have been more different from Mrs Clive in character. She was immensely sociable and went out of her way to meet new arrivals in the district. A close friend of Mrs Reiss, Dame Sylvia Crowe, recalls her discussing some newcomers with Mrs Fish which reflects something of their characters, 'I think they are a nice young couple', said Mrs Reiss. 'Yes, I suppose they are,' said Mrs Fish, 'but they have the most terrible soil.' Although Mrs Fish and Mrs Reiss shared a consuming interest in gardening, they also enjoyed one and other's company and the friendship deepened when they became widows. As with Mrs Clive, Mrs Fish went plant-hunting with Mrs Reiss; often they found treasures in derelict rectory gardens or from villagers who still gardened in the traditional cottage garden manner.

Dame Sylvia Crowe remembers an occasion when Mrs Fish was urging Mrs Reiss to accept a special plant but Mrs Reiss refused, saying 'Thank you so much Margery but I haven't got the right place for it.' She insisted on immaculate standards of upkeep and order and gardened energetically alongside her gardeners; her maxim was 'Never put in a plant unless there is a reason for it.' In theory Mrs Fish admired this approach: 'It is a mistake to allow too much sentiment in the garden. To have a really good garden the gardener must learn to throw away unwanted plants. That is one job I find most difficult, and an overpopulated garden is the result.' She was never disciplined when it came to the acquisition of plants. Her love of them meant that she was always adding to her collection as she discovered, and was seduced by, yet another variety.

Mrs Reiss was, according to Mrs Fish, a supreme 'groupist' (she regarded herself as a 'plantist'), a brilliant designer, devising schemes for her garden that placed great emphasis on colour and the arrangement of various forms of plants to produce a feeling of serenity – for her the all-important ingredient of a garden. A sample of Mrs Reiss's skill is described by Mrs Fish: '... a wide planting of *Stachys lanata* links the paving round the pond with the four formal beds planted with tall lilies, *Galtonia candicans*, *Artemisia* 'Silver Queen' and the froth of *Cineraria maritima*.' Whenever she and Mrs Fish visited other gardens, Mrs Reiss insisted on finding a seat where she would sit quietly to absorb the atmosphere. In her own garden she placed seats at strategic points so her visitors could do the same. Writing of Tintinhull in 1965, Mrs Fish paid tribute to the garden's atmosphere: 'Many gardens are interesting and beautiful, but few have this blessed feeling of serenity, for, whatever the season, the garden is lovely, with different flowers and shapes but always in harmony. This is achieved by choosing plants that fit in with a preconceived plan and not because of their individual attraction. This does not mean there are not unusual plants in the garden. There are many, but they have been chosen so cleverly that one sees the garden as a whole first and discovers the many treasures in it afterwards.'

Although Mrs Reiss's approach was more formal than Mrs Fish's, she understood how to grow plants in a natural way, making the most of the variety of conditions in her garden. In particular, Mrs Fish admired the way she used plants as ground cover. She noted Mrs Reiss's original way of using *Lathyrus lati-folius* as ground cover under a cedar. Also, in her notes for a book that was never published, she mentions how Mrs Reiss used *Cotoneaster horizontalis*: '... as a great feature of this garden, it is used as low plantings on beds and against the house, and makes a host for *Tropaeolum speciosum*.' She goes on to describe the use of periwinkles, *Viola labradorica*, *Geranium macrorrhizum* and alpine strawberries as underplanting in shaded areas.

Through her friendship with Mrs Reiss and Mrs Clive, Mrs Fish got to know other keen gardeners. One was Lady May Amory who lived at Chevithorne Barton near Tiverton. Her woodland garden, as described by Mrs Fish gives a glimpse of her art: 'Tall native pines furnish the woodland garden ... and Lady Amory has cleverly diverted a narrow stream to encircle it. Tall primulas grow at the edge of the water, there are bluebells and geraniums under the trees, with euphorbias, bergenias and Solomon's Seal. Beds raised with peat walls were specially constructed to give a selection of lilies the drainage and soil they need and many rare woodland plants are given the special conditions they like ... Monkshood is planted in big drifts, and in the autumn beautiful blue hydrangeas make big and sprawling bushes. Winter has its attraction for a large bush of *Mahonia japonica* scents the air, and the silver heads of honesty, grown in their hundreds, rustle gently. The garden has many unusual plants and it is planted with very great talent, yet one feels that nature has provided the abundance and it still has the hushed mystery of a coppice untouched by hand.' Lady Amory loved old roses and had masses of double primroses and perhaps was responsible for starting Mrs Fish off with her own collection.

Miss Nellie Britton and her sisters lived in a cottage beside the Knightshayes estate near Tiverton and grew many interesting and unusual plants. They visited New Zealand regularly and brought back specimen plants to try in their own garden. Mrs

Fish became an admirer of their collection which included many less well-known British herbaceous plants and, as time went on, she and the sisters swapped plants avidly. Certainly, she first saw *Euphorbia robbiae* in their garden: 'I first noticed it in Miss Nellie Britton's garden where it was growing under a hedge at the far end of the garden ... Here the euphorbia hid the untidy hedge and suppressed the various weeds the hedge encouraged. Miss Britton was a very great gardener and she knew the right plant for every place.'

The late James Platt, a great plantsman and former editorial assistant on the *Journal* of the Royal Horticultural Society, first met Mrs Fish in the late 1940s and encouraged her to broaden the range of her planting. It was he who suggested that she experiment with a wide range of acid-loving plants in the peat bed beside the ditch. Later, Mrs Fish began to doubt the value of creating an acid soil area on this site and abandoned planting lime-haters here. However, she had two small beds, one peat and one greensand, beside the house where she grew fine and rare plants that enjoyed acid conditions in a damp and shady situation. Gentians thrived here – *Gentiana × macaulayi*, *G. sino-ornata* and *G.* 'Inverleith'. *Iris cristata* which had refused to grow in full sun settled happily here and pleiones, known to be difficult and which until then she had never managed to keep, survived the winters, an achievement that prompted her to write: 'One of the joys of gardening is the occasional unexpected success after consistent failure.' Another treasure was *Kirengeshoma palmata*, an elegant herbaceous plant which Mrs Fish described as having 'that distinction and grace so often found in Japanese plants.' Navelwort, *Omphalodes luciliae*, is a delightful member of the forget-me-not family with grey-green leaves and soft blue flowers. Contrary to the accepted way of growing it in well-drained alkaline soil, Mrs Fish found that it grew much better in greensand. Despite her success with her acid beds, generally she thought it was better to restrict herself to plants that would grow easily in her own soil. She explained her reasons for this: 'To get the best results I am sure the wise thing is to stick to plants that grow well in one's particular soil. By various ways it is sometimes possible to keep unhappy plants alive for some time but they will die in the end and, as there are so many other good plants that will do well, it is foolish not to concentrate on them.'

During the many visits he made to East Lambrook, Mr Platt also made suggestions about planting shrubs and some rarer herbaceous plants, introducing Mrs Fish to the lovely early double delphinium 'Alice Artindale' and the spectacular kniphofia, 'Prince Igor.' He had a large collection of double primroses and was happy to give her some when he realised just how good a gardener she was becoming. Until 1963 there were a large number of double primrose varieties circulating among collectors, many having been saved from extinction in cottage gardens, but in that year dozens were wiped out by a virus. Mr Platt recalled with pleasure Mrs Fish's straightforward and unpretentious nature; when she had become a well-known gardener with several books published, she forbade him ever to buy one. Recognising his pre-eminence as a plantsman, she said simply, 'They are not for you.' Mr Platt found her garden in its heyday tremendously exciting – catholic in its diversity and not only aesthetically pleasing but also revolutionary. Although, with his wide experience, he knew most of its plants, the amateur gardening public did not. The plants and the way they were used introduced many people to a new concept of gardening. Mrs Fish's emphasis on herbaceous plants that needed minimum care – little or no staking, a long flowering period and the ability to spread as ground cover – challenged established ideas. The time had come for subtlety and closer consideration of individual plants.

During World War II the Fishes continued to garden, consolidating what they had created so far and coping with the lack of labour, but they were restricted from travelling to nurseries and interesting gardens at any great distance by petrol rationing.

It was in 1943 that Mrs. Fish first met Lanning Roper. He was a young American naval officer who arrived at East Lambrook with a letter of introduction from Bruce Buttfield, Margery's American cousin. His immense charm and easy manner endeared him to the Fishes and he became a frequent visitor to the Manor. Lanning Roper had been interested in plants long before he came to England, and already had a vague idea that he would make a career in horticulture, so he was more than willing to accompany Margery when she suggested visits to the best gardens in the area. Although there is no evidence that her gardening style influenced the way he designed gardens subsequently, undoubtedly he learnt much from her and she from him. Even as early as the latter part of the war when Mrs Fish had only been gardening for about five years, she already knew a great deal and had much to teach him. In time he often used plants in his designs that he had first seen at East Lambrook, particularly euphorbias and artemisias. In turn, he made her aware of some outstanding American plants rarely found in English gardens at that time. *Garrya elliptica*, *Magnolia grandiflora*, *Romneya coulteri* and *Carpenteria californica* were some of his favourites that later Mrs Fish grew and wrote about. Where he and she were particularly in accord was in their love of the wild flowers of their respective countries. Lanning Roper had fond memories of trilliums, terrestrial orchids (cypripediums), hepaticas, Virginian cowslip (*Mertensia virginica*), bloodroot (*Sanguinaria canadensis*) and *Aquilegia canadensis* growing wild in the woods beside the Hudson and the lakes of New England during his childhood. When he started designing gardens on this side of the Atlantic, they featured prominently in his informal schemes, alongside traditional English plants that he liked; lily-of-the-valley, bluebells and London pride. Once she became a knowledgeable gardener, Mrs Fish grew many American plants herself and helped to introduce them to a wider audience. She liked the Virginian cowslip very much, describing it as one of the loveliest spring plants and wrote lyrically of bloodroot – 'its lovely blue-grey leaves would make it worth growing without the snowy flowers with their glowing golden anthers. Some plants lose something when they have double flowers but bloodroot becomes even more beautiful.' As Lanning Roper became a well known garden designer his visits to East Lambrook became less frequent, but he and Mrs Fish remained friends for the rest of her life.

By the end of the war, although Margery was well aware that Walter's health was failing it still came as a shock to her when he had a heart attack and died suddenly on December 21st 1947. She reveals her sense of loss in notes she made for a biography she intended to write but never finished: 'I found it hard to believe that the scattering of a few ashes in a windswept crematorium garden in Weymouth one wintery morning could be the end of such an outstanding figure. He was so different from the ordinary run of people that I could not believe that anything so ordinary as death could happen to him.'

Realising that she needed a distraction from her grief, Mrs

Fish's family and friends persuaded her to accept an invitation from her American cousins, the Buttfields, to visit New Jersey, in 1948. Although, she had worked in Washington with Lord Northcliffe's War Mission at the end of World War I, her duties had prevented her from exploring the United States. Her 1948 visit was, therefore, her real introduction to the country and she enjoyed it so much that she made two more visits over the next three years. On this first trip her cousin, Bruce Buttfield, together with Lanning Roper, arranged a programme of garden tours in New Jersey and Pennsylvania. The beauty of the landscape, the scope and style of American gardens and the range of the architecture deeply impressed Mrs Fish. She was especially impressed by the gardens of Dumbarton Oaks which introduced her to the work of Beatrix Farrand, perhaps the greatest of all American garden designers. Mrs Farrand spent some time in England before World War II, designing the garden at Dartington Hall – a favourite of Mrs Fish's.

One of Mrs Farrand's contributions to gardening was the work she did on the use of ground cover plants. She experimented with hundreds around her home in Maine and used them extensively in all her designs, long before the idea caught on in Britain. Mrs Fish came to embrace Mrs Farrand's ideas wholeheartedly and became the leading exponent of the value of ground cover. One of her lasting impressions of ground cover in America was the use of *Pachysandra terminalis*: 'This is the plant the Americans use to make carpets of green under their trees. In so many American gardens the natural trees are left and simply underplanted with pachysandra and English ivy and certainly the effect is pleasing and furnished at all times of the year.'

By 1951 Mrs Fish had come to terms with the loss of her husband and with her solitary existence. She was able to turn all her energies to her career as a writer and gardener and to perfect her ideas of cottage gardening at East Lambrook Manor. Her life was now entering its most productive and rewarding years.

5

The Mature Garden
in Winter and Spring

'Gardening is like everything else in life, you get out of it as much as you put in ... You must love it and then your love will be repaid a thousand fold, as every gardener knows.'

FROM THE EARLY 1950s gardening became the focus of Mrs Fish's life. It was in this period that the garden at East Lambrook assumed its distinctive character and became one of the most influential gardens in England. Essentially, it always remained a cottage garden but became increasingly sophisticated in the range of plants grown, although the layout and spirit of the garden remained the same. By the time it had reached its zenith, in the late 1950s, Mrs Fish had amassed an enormous number of plants and arranged them with the greatest skill, yet she never succumbed to indiscriminate plant acquisition. She was not afraid to move a plant until she had found the perfect spot for it – aiming primarily to provide the best growing conditions and secondarily to produce a harmonious effect. Furthermore, she had mastered the art of making the garden interesting throughout the year. At this time, before her writing and lecturing commitments became too demanding, she was able, with some part-time help, to keep the garden in immaculate condition. She thought that there was no excuse for untidiness. It would be quite wrong to think of Mrs Fish's style of gardening as a licence for laziness. And it was only in the last few years of her life, with her

.Margery Fish started her gardening odyssey at East Lambrook Manor when she was already 46 years old. Even in her 70's, as seen here, she continued to garden, write and lecture with the same contagious enthusiasm.

There was no structure and few plants in the garden when Walter and Margery Fish came to East Lambrook in 1938. This 1950's photograph shows the immature planting of the sundial garden and barton, with the *Acer pseudoplatanus* 'Leopoldii' on the main lawn beyond.

A view of the main lawn in the 1960's shows how skilful Mrs Fish had become at producing an overall effect. Valerian and *Artemisia absinthium* 'Lambrook Silver' seen here in the foreground, and angelica in the herb garden, demonstrate her aptitude for placing a plant in the right position.

From the start, it was Mrs Fish's intention that the garden should complement the old hamstone house. Seen here in the 1960's, the path to the main entrance has been given a softening fringe of angelica, *Geranium pratense, Euphorbia myrsinites* and *Gladiolus communis byzantinus*.

The same area of the garden today, from the centre of the barton. Mrs Fish's ideal of close planting and informal style remains, but more robust plants have been used. In the foreground, *Hebe* 'Margery Fish' (now *H.* 'Primley Gem') contrasts with the polished foliage of a large-leaved ivy and the delicate tracery of fennel. Behind the hebe, a sumach – *Rhus typhina laciniata* – spreads along the wall at the edge of the lawn.

Rhus typhina laciniata, whose finely-cut leaves are seen here in their October colour, was planted after Mrs Fish's death in 1969. She would have approved of its contribution to the Autumn garden.

In the early 1960's, Mrs Fish gave every moment she could to maintain the delicate balance of her planting. Here, romping around the lawn's edging wall, is *Erigeron karvinskianus* which has now been replaced by the sumach. The tree in the foreground is a *Rhus potaninii*.

The ruby leaves of the *Rhus potaninii* make a dazzling, but brief, display in October.

Mrs Fish took pleasure in her garden all through the year. She left
many of her herbaceous plants uncut, as this old picture shows,
because she enjoyed the winter silhouettes of dessicated seed heads,
stalks and leaves.

In this contemporary photograph, the soft pinks of astrantias and
geraniums mingle with the foliage of irises and a mullein. Across the
lawn is the long border, now shaded by mature trees.

An early photograph of the terrace garden in spring illustrates how open the terraces were and how complex the planting needed to be to achieve Mrs Fish's aim of making them look attractive from all sides and at all times of the year. The summerhouse – once the privy – can be seen behind the cherry tree.

Much the same view later in the season. Mrs Fish often used gold and silver foliage as a foil for her brighter coloured cottage plants. In the foreground are the silver and yellow spikes of *Verbascum rotundifolium haensleri*.

The terrace garden today, seen from the summerhouse. There is now no overall view across the terraces as the trees and shrubs have grown to maturity. It is hoped that as restoration continues, a more open aspect will be regained.

Today, *Angelica archangelica* is as much a decorative feature of the herb garden as it was in Mrs Fish's time.

Close planting has always been the essence of the garden. Here, the foliage of bergenias, euphorbia and grasses enjoy the shade of the variegated sycamore and *Cornus controversa* 'Variegata'.

Mrs Fish's 'pudding' trees – *Chamaecyparis lawsoniana* 'Fletcheri' – seen here in the 1960's, were planted along the crooked path running up through the terrace garden, to provide its main axis. Their strong shape acted as a foil for the plants grown around them, such as the *Penstemon heterophyllus* in the foreground.

Today, the 'pudding' trees are much larger than in Mrs Fish's time, although they were replaced in 1971. The present owners are considering replacing them again.

Mrs Fish stressed the importance of an evergreen framework for any garden. A present-day view of the house
from the terrace path shows this ideal demonstrated in
the planting of *Skimmia japonica*, euphorbias, ivies, golden
box and various conifers.

An old view of the terraces, looking towards the malthouse, displays Mrs Fish's talent for placing plants of all
kinds in pleasing relationships. As she once wrote of her
style of gardening; 'to be a success the planting has to be
mixed, with shrubs, irises, bulbous plants and foliage
plants.'

Mrs Fish introduced some plants into her garden that became menaces as they seeded prolifically. One was *Astrantia major*, of which she wrote in 1967: 'Of recent years astrantias have become a real problem, but the progeny are all lovely'.

In the borders, Mrs Fish grew both old and new roses, but always as part of a mixed planting scheme.

A 1960's photograph of the path leading to the summerhouse illustrates Mrs Fish's preference for plants that billow over the edges of walls, paths and beds.

Looking north towards the summerhouse, *Cornus controversa* 'Variegata' now shades the end of the lower terrace path with its edging of roses, catmint and pinks.

Mrs Fish advocated 'jungle' gardening, in which plants are allowed to intermingle as in nature while being set within an ordered framework. Echoes of her ideas are seen in this contemporary photograph.

Blue-silver thimbles
of the free-seeding
Eryngium giganteum
stand out against
the dense foliage of
a 'pudding' tree.

. . . as does purple-
eyed *Euphorbia
characias*.

These photographs show the same view of the house and terrace garden. In the earlier one, strong definition is given by the small conifers and the broad spectrum of colour used. Today, what is lost in structure and colour variation is compensated by a subtlety of foliage texture and shape.

Plants jostle for position in the lowest terrace beds. In the foreground, *Nectaroscordum siculum* – a favourite of Mrs Fish's – hangs its delicate pink and green bells.

A section of the long border as it was in early summer at the beginning of the 1960's. Then it was dominated by several silver thistles – *Cynara cardunculus* – whose architectural foliage stood out against the roses grown up poles along the border's length.

A winding path behind the malthouse entices the visitor towards the ditch garden. It was Mrs Fish's intention that the garden should be enticing and it still retains this quality.

Although Mrs Fish used silver-leaved plants throughout the garden, in the mid-1960's, when this photograph was taken, she created a small silver garden to house a wider variety of unusual and 'difficult' plants.

Today, newer varieties of silver plants continue to be added but self-seeders, like the alliums and wild mulleins, are made welcome.

Among the silver garden's present inhabitants are white lavender, *Dorycnium hirsutum*, *Iris pallida* 'Argentea Variegata', various helichrysums and artemisias with yellow-flowered asphodels in the background.

A study in silver and pink with *Dianthus* 'Lilian' and the rose 'Great Maiden's Blush' against the silver garden's surrounding hedge of *Lonicera nitida*.

Mrs Fish clothed every available wall with carefully chosen creepers and climbers, but did not like them to obscure their brick or stone background. Today, self-seeded valerian, alpine strawberries, spurges and white comfrey produce a soft edging to the roadside wall.

When the front garden was repaved under Walter Fish's supervision, the effect was too neat for Margery's taste and she surreptitiously attacked the concrete bedding with a crowbar. 'All manner of creeping things' were planted in the resulting gaps to create, as seen here, a living carpet.

It is now impossible to
have the same controlled
effect, as the wall shrubs,
climbers and self-sown
plants cascade over much
of the paved area.

Today's cottage garden
effect is provided by a
mixture of traditional and
modern plants. *Penstemon*
'White Bedder', a pink
cistus and cranesbill
complement the giant
hollyhock, *Rosa* 'Great
Maiden's Blush' and
wisteria framing the door.

The sundial garden, beside the cowshed, seen in spring when it is a mass of hellebores, daffodils and iris leaves.

Although the sundial garden and upper rockery outside the malthouse have yet to be restored, they still make a pleasing picture in early summer.

As summer progresses, it becomes a haze of *Geranium pratense* seedlings, campanulas, rock roses and foliage of the perennial sweet pea.

One of the two south-facing rockeries Mrs Fish made in her early gardening days. In the 1950's, when this photograph was taken, she was already experimenting with the softening effect of silver plants on more strident colours. She never felt restricted to growing only alpines and in her later years she used shrubs and spreaders more extensively.

Monarda didyma 'Croftway Pink' and the variegated foliage of *Phlox paniculata* 'North Leigh' are to be found today by the path behind the malthouse.

The original palm tree – *Trachycarpus fortunei* – and a blue cedar dominate the green garden in winter, while three of Mrs Fish's favourite families – bergenias, spurges and periwinkles – provide foliage interest throughout the bleakest months.

By late spring, a more ethereal picture is created. Here, the delicate white flowers of *Cercis siliquastrum* 'Alba' overhang part of the green garden.

Spring in the ditch garden in Mrs Fish's day. She realised that its damp and shaded situation was the perfect habitat for primroses and snowdrops.

The dramatic foliage of a skunk cabbage – *Lysichiton americanus* – contrasts with cottage garden flowers in the Lido in spring.

The Lido in early summer takes on an exotic quality. The dense planting includes ornamental rhubarbs, skunk cabbages, rodgersias and a white wisteria.

Mrs Fish's original planting in the Lido illustrates her skill in choosing the right plants for a harmonious 'jungle' effect.

Mrs Fish amassed an enormous collection of hellebores in part of the old orchard beside the ditch. Since her time, they have hybridized, making identification difficult.

Pollarded willows are still a traditional feature of Somerset ditches. Their stark shape contrasts with the *Hamamelis mollis* whose sulphur-yellow flowers were valued by Mrs Fish for their contribution to the late winter scene.

A picture of the ditch in March shows how many primroses have been reintroduced during the last few years.

Like the Lido, in
early summer the
ditch takes on a very
different character,
when an overall
effect is more
important than the
individual plants.

(*Below*) In Mrs
Fish's day, as seen
here, there was
greater definition of
colour and form
within the late
summer ditch
garden.

Whatever the time of year, there are plants of character to be found. Here, the spring-flowering *Trillium sessile* thrives on the banks of the ditch garden.

'No other flower seems quite so much at home in the cottage garden as does the primrose', Mrs Fish wrote in *Cottage Garden Flowers*. They were one of her first loves and over the years she built up an enviable collection.

In early spring
there is an air of
enchantment in the
orchard garden.
Mrs Fish's now
mature shrubs and
trees cast dappled
shade over an
informal carpet of
spring flowers.

Summer heightens
the magical quality
within the orchard
garden as the
sunlight, filtering
through the deep
shade, accentuates
the texture and
shape of the foliage
plants.

Mrs Fish took her responsibilities as a garden writer seriously and followed a strict daily routine at her desk as well as in the garden.

health weakening, that she was unable to keep to her rigorous standards.

By the late 1950s and early 1960s many of the trees and shrubs were mature, but in balance with the vast amount of herbaceous plants around them. The immense variety of plants and their arrangement throughout the garden were sources of inspiration to the many people who now came to visit East Lambrook. Derek Tilley, who as picture editor of *The Field* photographed the garden on many occasions, thinks that 'the garden was full of ideas for other gardeners. It made them feel they could garden as they wanted, instead of having bowling-green lawns and perfect beds of this and that. William Robinson originated the idea, but Mrs Fish brought it up to date and popularised it.' He remembers an occasion at East Lambrook when he noticed visitors so overcome by the garden that they were 'whispering in awe.'

With almost twenty years of gardening experience behind her, Mrs Fish had by this time become such an accomplished gardener that she was able to approach all areas of her garden with equal confidence – no site was too difficult. There was a dense concentration of plants throughout the garden, every bit of ground richly covered. The walls of the house and outbuildings were clothed with climbing plants, many rare, and a profusion of plants spilled out of the beds on to the paths and over the low retaining walls. It appeared as if every bit of space had been used to maximum effect and there could not possibly be room for any more introductions. In fact Mrs Fish went on acquiring plants and placing them with sensitivity in her living tapestry right up until her death.

The use of the hoe, except in the vegetable garden, was never allowed at East Lambrook after Walter died. All the weeding was done by hand and seedlings carefully inspected for their value. If they were good plants, in the right place, they were allowed to remain, adding to the controlled profusion. Mrs Fish knew she could depend on them to fill gaps and add colour: 'In any garden that is well filled with the natural type of plant – species rather than hybrids – a large number of seedlings come up year after year. I rely on many of them to help fill the garden, and am grateful for this source of treasure.'

From the start of her gardening days, Mrs Fish realised the importance of finding a site for a plant best suited to its needs.

Graham Stuart Thomas, another frequent visitor to the garden in its heyday, remembers its enormous range of plants and believes that these were grown so successfully because there were so many different sites and soils available. The groundwork to produce the various habitats had been done in Walter's time: the terraced garden for a mixture of herbaceous material, bulbs and shrubs; the paths and low stone walls for plants that liked a dry or restricted root run; the ditch garden for those needing a damp and shaded site; and the rockeries for alpine plants. The peat and greensand areas, as well as the troughs and raised beds, also allowed Mrs Fish to experiment with an even wider selection. Furthermore, she went to great lengths to improve the heavy clay soil, digging and mulching with as much organic material as she could find. In some parts of the garden, however, the soil never really improved and so she chose plants that did not mind clay. Roses, clematis, campanulas, hellebores, primroses and hostas were some of the plants that tolerated it.

Today, Mrs Fish is remembered and revered for the contribution she made to several fields of gardening; principally as a conserver and populariser of cottage garden plants, but also as a proponent of the all-the-year garden as well as an innovator in the use of ground cover and as an expert in planting difficult sites. Her book *Gardening in the Shade* remains a bible to keen gardeners and was described, as recently as 1988, by Robin Lane Fox as the best on the subject. In Mrs Fish's lifetime, her garden became famous for its comprehensive collection of cottage garden plants, particularly geraniums, snowdrops, hellebores and euphorbias. However, during the 1950s and '60s, she also established collections of other plants she had come to admire like bergenias, penstemons, silver-leaved plants, species irises and cyclamen. As her knowledge grew, she delighted in accumulating even more unusual and esoteric subjects and developed a fascination for green flowers and variegated foliage. Plants with white flowers intrigued her and she sought out as many as she could find: 'White flowers have great charm and I'd like to have a white version of every flower in the garden.' However, the denizens of the cottage garden always remained high in her affection and she continued to refer to herself as a cottage gardener. She never tired of adding different forms of traditional cottage plants – violets, primroses, erigerons, campanulas, columbines, daisies and pinks were the kinds of things that had the charm and, at times, the challenge, that satisfied her. Her collector's zeal impressed many people, including her fellow gardener and writer, Anne Scott-James. In 1968 in an article in *Queen* called 'The Great Lady of Gardening', she wrote of East Lambrook, 'not only are the plants profuse, but their variety is enormous, for Mrs Fish likes to try form after form. It is pretty impressive to find a gardener growing seven forms of the lesser periwinkle.' These were *Vinca minor*, *V. m. alba*, *V. m. atropurpurea*, *V. m.* 'Argenteo-variegata', *V. m.* 'Azurea Flore Pleno', *V. m.* 'La Grave' and *V. m.* 'Multiplex'.

When her garden reached its maturity, Mrs Fish took great delight that it offered something of interest on every day of the year, not only all the things she had planned but unexpected happenings – a surprisingly early bloom, an old friend that she thought lost happily reappearing, or an accidental, but successful, plant grouping. Her writing reveals enthusiasm for every season and joy in its plants. The winter seemed to offer as much for her as did the height of summer. At a time when most gardeners put away their tools and retreat to the fireside to browse through catalogues in anticipation of next year's season, she spent as much time as she could in the garden, observing, planning and simply enjoying: 'I found the garden a very exciting place on this winter's day ... I love the flowers that bloom in the winter. Each one is a thrill and I think we get as much pleasure from one tiny bloom on a winter's day as we do from a gardenful of roses in summer.'

The beginning of the year was the time for snowdrops with their 'aloofness and purity.' Mrs Fish was always on the lookout for rare and interesting ones. Perhaps her interest in these under-stated little flowers was fostered by her admiration for E. A. Bowles, a great snowdrop expert. Writing in 1964, she pays tribute to him and the plantsman, Walter Butt, whose collections did so much to promote interest in snowdrops: 'Once interest has been aroused in the many variations of the common snowdrop and in other interesting species, winter is no longer dull and cold but becomes exciting as we watch for the different snowdrops to appear.' It was the double-flowered, green-centred 'Ophelia' that started her on the trail: 'Collecting snowdrops is a growing cult. We compare, covert and contrive to get new and exciting ones.' Most of her special varieties were grown in the ditch garden along the bottom of which visitors could walk. This meant that they were below the snowdrops because Mrs Fish believed that to see their real beauty, they needed to be planted at eye level or above. However, other species that required an open sunny position, such as *Galanthus gracilis* and *G. plicatus byzantinus*, as well the autumn flowering types, were grown in troughs, raised beds and the rock garden. Recognising the importance of not over-whelming their delicate beauty, Mrs Fish generally provided pulmonarias, hellebores and small variegated ivies as companions. However, she found that the rich crimson leaves of *Bergenia purpurascens* were lovely with clumps of the common snowdrop and *Galanthus elwesii* showed up well against the lac-quered foliage of × *Fatshedera lizei*.

By careful planning, Mrs Fish ensured that there were many other small flowers brightening dark winter days. Plants, fool-hardy enough to risk flowering at the most inhospitable time of year, always appealed to her and she cherished them as much as her snowdrops. Small species irises (such as *Iris histrioides sophenensis*, *I. unguicularis alba* and *I. u. angustifolia*), winter aconites, pulmonarias and the winter-flowering cyclamen like *C. coum*, *C. c.* 'Atkinsii' and *C. c. caucasicum* (*C. ibericum*) were sited where she could keep an eye on them and pampered to encourage them to spread. Cyclamen were especially precious: 'There are several reasons why cyclamen appeal to me so strongly. They are among the prettiest and daintiest flowers one can have, they come at times when there are not many flowers about, and they don't mind a bit where they grow.' One of Mrs Fish's early ambitions was to increase her stocks of autumn-flowering *Cyclamen hed-erifolium* and the spring-flowering *C. repandum* so that they would completely fill the ground beneath all the lonicera hedges in the garden. Also, as she liked to see them snuggling under the 'pudding trees' that lined the path through the terrace garden, she spent a good deal of time carefully moving seedlings here. As her stock of these plants increased, some were used to brighten up the bare earth among the roots of large trees and shrubs, but the rare varieties were cosseted in the rock garden and the troughs. Although Mrs Fish grew cyclamen that flowered in all seasons, it was the winter-flowering ones that she especially liked. A cerise-flowered *Cyclamen coum* gave her the greatest pleasure: 'To see *C. coum* in full flower on a winter's morning is something you'll never forget. It positively twinkles and sparkles in the winter sunshine.'

While the delicate beauty of these early flowers was very welcome, they would have looked lost without some background structure to the garden. It was to evergreens that Mrs Fish turned to provide the furnished look that is so necessary in winter and early spring: 'When I plan my garden, I try always to have enough evergreen plants to make an attractive structure throughout the year and tend to think more about the winter than the summer, because the summer really looks after itself.' Her most valued evergreens were shrubs like hollies, mahonias, *Choisya ternata*, skimmias, daphnes, elaeagnus, and a few slow-growing conifers. These stalwarts were used in all the areas of the garden and Mrs Fish took care to produce pleasing foliage pictures and not overwhelm the small winter-flowering plants. She believed that the beginning of the year is the time when it is most important to have harmonious groupings in the garden. Typical examples of these plantings were the placing of *Hebe* 'Spender's Seedling' with a skirt of *Euonymus fortunei radicans* against a backdrop of *Hedera helix* 'Parsley Crested' on the wall behind, and a purple-leaved filbert grown with a wide underplanting of *Euonymus fortunei* 'Silver Queen'.

Although she valued evergreens to dress the garden in winter, she also liked to see the bare shapes of deciduous trees. As her knowledge increased, her taste in trees became more discriminating and she added to those she and Walter had planted together. A *Cornus kousa chinensis* was planted in the higher ground to the west of the ditch garden and one of her favourite winter-flowering trees, *Prunus* x *subhirtella* 'Autumnalis', in the top lawn: 'I can think of no other tree that has a six month season.' Beside the top lawn she planted *Acer capillipes* for its good autumn colour and attractive striped bark. The larger Norway maple, *Acer platanoides* 'Goldsworth Purple' was sited in the long border beside the eastern boundary wall. *Magnolia grandiflora* 'Exmouth' had been an early choice for the white garden beyond the terrace garden but later she added *Magnolia stellata*. Near the Lido at the top of the garden, she planted *Amelanchier canadensis*, a valuable small tree for its white spring flowers and vivid autumn colouring.

To Mrs Fish, 'evergreen' had a much broader meaning than is generally understood by the term. She meant by it any foliage that helped to furnish the garden in the winter; not only the obvious shrubs, but also ferns, ivies, grasses and the coloured foliage of herbaceous plants. This included such things as the orange-russet leaves of *Geranium macrorrhizum*, and *Bergenia purpurascens*, the touches of silver from plants like *Helichrysum stoechas barrelieri* and *Verbascum bombyciferum* and the silvery trails of *Lamium galeobdolon* 'Variegatum'. She described the lamium as 'my answer to most ground cover problems.'

The starry flowers and glossy leaves of periwinkles, both green and variegated, were another valuable form of ground cover. Mrs Fish found they had many uses and encouraged others to try them. Although their heyday had been in Victorian times they were gaining in popularity when Mrs Fish started gardening, but they were still not very widely grown. At East Lambrook, dull or inhospitable sites were enlivened by their glistening foliage and early flowers; walls were turned into green and white waterfalls and the tendrils of the more restrained members of the genus like *Vinca difformis* were encouraged to twine about the branches of shrubs, bare in winter. Mrs Fish did not disdain the ordinary *V. minor*, shunned by many gardeners: 'It is so neat and industrious that it can be introduced into the highest society without apology.' She thought it the best for making a dense carpet and it could be lightened by having a variegated form growing through it. Her favourite form of all was *V. minor* 'La Grave', which she found could, if kept trimmed, be grown as a bushy herbaceous plant rather than as ground cover.

As well as the colours of flowers and the structure of evergreens, Mrs Fish attached great importance to scent in the winter garden: 'Scent in the garden is just as important, I think, as colour and form, scent at every time of the year and every time of the day.' Winter was the time for wintersweets, witchhazels, daphnes, viburnums and sarcococcas to flower and, although their flowers were not necessarily the showiest, they compensated by adding rich fragrance to the air.

It was not living plants only that made a contribution to the coldest and barest season. In some cases, the remains of the previous summer's herbaceous plants were considered valuable: 'Skeletons can be very telling. My garden is peopled by the bare stems of perennials and all the grasses, many of which are bleached to old ivory.' Against the solid backdrop of evergreen shrubs and coloured foliage, she liked to see the spires of dessicated flowers, silhouettes of seed pods and the filigree patterns of the branches of deciduous trees and shrubs. The move towards leaving plants untrimmed for the winter was certainly welcome; she liked to have bold dried flower and foliage arrangements in the house, so her 'deads', as she called them, served a dual purpose – to decorate both the house and the garden.

To Mrs Fish, hellebores were a vital component of her winter and spring garden. She loved them for their exquisitely-marked flowers and strong leaf shape: 'For an all-the-year-round garden there is nothing to beat them.' By regular feeding and giving them the conditions they liked best, she had flowers of different varieties from November to June and the benefit of their foliage for the rest of the year. The first to flower was *Helleborus orientalis olympicus* which opened its pale green buds in October, revealing large white flowers. *H. o. atrorubens* and *H. o. kochii* followed in November. The latter is considered to be the true orientalis hellebore, distinguishable from the hybrids by its large, coarsely-toothed leaves and delicate, nearly primrose-yellow flowers. Mrs Fish never did as well with the Christmas rose, *H. niger*, as other gardeners she knew. However, she did not abandon it completely, growing one of its pink-flowered forms, *H. niger macranthus*. This, with narrower leaves than the species and large pink-flushed flowers held on long stems above the leaves, was a favourite. Some of the hellebores have the added bonus of fragrant flowers, but Mrs Fish remarked that one would need to flatten oneself on the ground to appreciate the slight scent of the green flowers of *H. odorus*, a hellebore that flowered for her before Christmas.

She grew some of her orientalis hellebores in the paved front garden where they took over the scene from the hydrangeas in the late autumn. Many others were grown in the orchard beds, some with polyanthus and *Primula sieboldii* for company, others with cultivated grasses and bergenias. The purple-ruby flowered *H. orientalis abchasicus* was grown here. In time, Mrs Fish acquired a number of plants of this hellebore from various sources and found that they were all slightly different. Her plants of *H. orientalis guttatus* also varied in their white or greenish-pink blooms, heavily spotted with maroon inside. She tried hard to keep her orientalis children in separate colour groups – a time-consuming enterprise that would try the patience of any gardener, so prolific and varied were their progeny. Many grew on top of the ditch banks and in shaded, raised beds, so the flowers' interior markings could be studied. Although Mrs Fish did not grow the native, poisonous *H. foetidus*, in its wild form she did grow two other forms; the 'Italian form' and another, finer unnamed one, both of which she attributed to E. A. Bowles. These were planted under her silver birch trees on the top lawn behind a grouping of a low-growing juniper, golden sage and *Iris foetidissima*.

There were two hellebores that Mrs Fish liked above all others. *H. argutifolius* (syn. *H. lividus corsicus*) was admired for its beautiful serrated foliage and clusters of palest green, cupped flowers. It was given pride of place in the front garden and, to make a fine green winter picture, planted with the tender *Euphorbia mellifera* and *E. characias wulfenii*. She also found that phormiums, with their stiff strap-like leaves, made good contrasts for it. Her other favourite was *H. cyclophyllus*, a larger, more handsome version of *H. odorus*, with pure green flowers in February. Although Mrs Fish admired *H. lividus* for its grey-laced leaves and scented pinkish-green flowers in early spring, like many gardeners, she found it tender and temperamental and resorted to growing it in pots placed in the front garden for the spring and summer, shaded by *Garrya elliptica*. Another treasured member of the genus, *H. x sternii* came from the Porlock garden of the renowned plantsman, Norman Hadden. There were several plants of the deciduous *H. purpurascens* and its hybrid *H. torquatus* (of gardens) at East Lambrook, all with slightly different colouring of their blue-purple flowers. The last hellebore to flower, sometimes from March to June, was the other English native, *H. viridis*, with its small, brilliant-green blooms. When Mrs Fish discovered the virtues of hellebores, she set about trying to interest her readers in them: 'No plants are better suited to the shady garden than the hellebores, for they need a shady site and are wonderful plants for growing under deciduous shrubs and trees and under north walls.' Hellebores were an important ingredient, too, of the green garden which she made in 1966. Here, with many euphorbias, astrantias, *Alchemilla mollis* and *A. alpina*, she mixed the evergreen *Bupleurum fruticosum*, *Ribes laurifolium* with greenish-yellow flowers and winter-flowering sarcococcas, *Daphne laureola* and the fern-leaved *Clematis cirrhosa balearica*: 'I don't suppose we would look twice at its rather nondescript flowers in the summer, but they are pleasant at this time of year.'

As the coldest days of the year gave way to the warmer, but wet and windy, days of March and April, groups of daffodils brought much more emphatic colour to the garden: 'When one thinks of old daffodils it is usually the double ones that come first to mind. They have an old world air and are the kind that seem to thrive without attention, and so we find them in the little old gardens that have daffodils next to the cabbages and tulips among the currants.' As a cottage gardener, Mrs Fish grew several old double narcissi, including *N*. 'Queen Anne's Double' and the double pheasant's eye, *N. poeticus* 'Flore Pleno' but she did not neglect single varieties, like the single pheasant's eye, *N. poeticus recurvus*. Generally she preferred the paler, less bold varieties. As well as a profusion of daffodils, it was the enormous numbers of primroses in the garden that most strikingly marked the transition from winter to spring.

Mrs Fish started collecting them almost as soon as she started gardening: 'No other flower seems quite so much at home in the cottage garden as does the primrose.' However, like many other gardeners she found some, particularly those with double flowers, not easy to keep, but this did not deter her: 'If you start collecting primroses, there is no end to it.' She grew singles, doubles, Jacks-in-the-green, hose-in-hose varieties, polyanthus and auriculas. The list is remarkably long, but sadly many of the varieties she tried so hard to save are thought to have disappeared from cultivation. Among her favourites was the small single green primrose which she described as being 'very old and terribly scarce.' She loved the old eyeless primrose, 'Bartimaeus,' and a favourite polyanthus of the cottage garden, 'Barrowby Gem', with its 'pure, pale lemon flowers, green-eyed and deliciously scented.' These two were especially welcome because they flowered so early in the year. Unlike some other gardeners, she did not despise *Primula* 'Wanda': 'quite lovely used naturally and inconspicuously.' She especially liked the pale lilac-flowered *Primula elatior meyeri* 'Grandiflora' (*P. altaica grandiflora*) – 'entrancingly clean and gentle in the early spring.' Of the double primroses, she suggested that the easiest five to grow were *P. vulgaris* 'Alba Plena', *P. v.* 'Lilacina Plena', 'Marie Crousse', 'Bon Accord Gem' and 'Our Pat'. At East Lambrook, these were planted in the shade of tall perennials in loamy soil, enriched with old cow manure, each bunch surrounded by flat stones. To ensure their good health, Mrs Fish gave them a tonic of wood ash, plenty of water in hot weather and divided them between October and April. Although she lost many doubles over the years, she did manage to keep the dark velvety red 'Madame de Pompadour,' despite its being, 'as unpredictable as that of the lady whose name she bears.'

Auriculas also proved difficult at times: 'like so many other flowers, I think they do best for the people who do not fuss over them too much ... In my anxiety to please them I usually cannot resist over-feeding.' She tried the smaller varieties – *P. marginata* and *P.* × *pubescens* in many different positions in shade and sun in a variety of soils, but they were never truly at home. Hose-in-hose and Jacks-in-the-green primroses, many of which date from the 16th century, were always a struggle and Mrs Fish, like many others, bemoaned the disappearance of so many named varieties. Among the candelabra primulas, the clear, cool yellow *P. prolifera* and the primrose-coloured *P. florindae* (giant cowslip) were favourites for their easy natures – she discovered that she could grow them in sites that were not necessarily damp. *P. rosea* with its uncompromising pink colouring, did not fit in with other flowers and had to have the scene to itself, while *P. denticulata*, the drumstick primula, was recommended for its ease and effectiveness with other plants. She experimented with others that would grow only in peat: *P. clarkei*, with its tiny rose flowers and coppery-crimson leaves, *P. forrestii*, *P. pulverulenta* 'Bartley Strain' and *P. chionantha*. However, against the recommended way of growing the petiolaris group in a lime-free bed, she grew them in ordinary soil enriched with leafmould. With her characteristic energy, Mrs Fish always carried a spade and a sack in the back of the car and collected leafmould whenever she came across a suitable source. There were times when she would stop and fill her sack even though she was in evening clothes on her way to or from a party. She may have grown many rarified varieties of the primula family, and tried hard to please them, but it was the simple wayside flower that, above all, she loved best: 'Although I love all the little coloured primroses, none of them is so artlessly lovely as the wild primrose.'

In the same way that the common primrose was the forerunner of the garden cultivars, so too the little violet of the hedgerows and woodland was the ancestor of many of those we grow today.

Mrs Fish noted that in the cottagers' gardens, violets 'just arrive, but they don't get in anyone's way; in fact, I think they are a very welcome form of ground cover, and their sweetness is there for all who'll take it.' Violas did well for her – the more prolific seeders too well sometimes. A particular favourite was *V. cornuta*, which she described as having 'small flowers that are as graceful as butterflies.' *Viola labradorica purpurea* was recommended as excellent ground cover, its only fault being that it had no scent. Among the species, she also grew the rarer *V. biflora* and *V. pensylvanica*. Of the cultivated varieties, the single forms and their seedlings particularly appealed to her and she considered *V.* 'Coeur d'Alsace', in warm pink, the loveliest of all: 'I find it so delightful to find these heavenly-scented, heavenly-coloured little flowers blooming away in the depths of winter.' Among the other varieties she liked were the red-purple 'Admiral Avellan', the claret-coloured 'Red Queen' and the blue 'John Raddenbury'; this last she found useful as an underplanting for roses in full sun. Being a disciple of E. A. Bowles, naturally she had his black viola, and told her readers that it looked especially good among silver foliage. A friendly antique dealer gave her her first double violet, 'Duchesse de Parme', and this was followed by the deep lavender-flowered 'Marie Louise' and 'Swanley White'.

A plant was never too small or insignificant to merit Mrs Fish's interest if it intrigued her or she thought it ought to be preserved. She was especially fond of understated plants that required close scrutiny to appreciate their charms. However, seemingly at odds with this preference, she had an enduring passion for spurges. As the garden matured, the bold strong shapes and bright colour of the larger members of the family became characteristic features of its landscape. When Mrs Fish started gardening in the late 1930s, very few people collected them. E. A. Bowles was an exception and it was probably his advocacy that opened her eyes to their charm and usefulness. Once she started to acquire them herself, she became addicted: 'The first euphorbia planted in the garden is usually the forerunner of many more. For there is something about these strange green-flowered plants that appeals to one's collecting instincts. Luckily there are many of them, and it is safe to say that for every position in the garden there is a suitable euphorbia.' Mrs Fish was full of praise for these accommodating plants. The evergreen ones are eye-catching in winter with their crooked shapes and as spring approaches they gradually uncurl their limbs to show off profuse bracts of starry 'eyed' flowers. The deciduous varieties appear in the spring with foliage of greenish-yellow or vivid green that brings long-lasting pleasure to the garden: 'We have discovered the value of their magnificent foliage, which is beautiful on every day in the year.'

Mrs Fish's introduction to the spurges was *E. characias wulfenii sibthorpii* which has a dark brown eye at the centre of its flowering yellow bracts. For a hardy, evergreen plant *E. c. wulfenii*, the largest and earliest flowering of the group, was Mrs Fish's favourite. She had her original cutting from Mr Butt's garden. In one place at East Lambrook, it looked handsome when grown in a 'green' scheme with the bronze-tinted leaves of *E. mellifera* and *Helleborus argutifolius* (syn. *H. lividus corsicus*): 'Flowers may come and flowers may go, but that handsome mass of glaucous foliage will be there as a foil and a furnishing and a refreshment for many years.' Mrs Fish used the black-eyed *E. characias* in several places to good effect. One of its chance seedlings produced a particularly good yellow form that she propagated and subsequently named 'Lambrook Gold'. She found that the taller types looked best planted in a corner where their long limbs could be contained. Another tall spurge she liked is *E. sikkimensis*, with brilliant red stems and tinted leaves. Later in the season, the leaves become green with white veins and the 'flowers' take the form of 'lovebird' green bracts. Mrs Fish thought it was very useful for growing under trees and between shrubs. The Irish spurge, *E. hyberna* came from a friend's garden but only with some difficulty. Mrs Fish recalled how the innocent-looking seedling had to be prised from the ground with a tyre lever! Once in its new home it settled down to make dazzling greenish-gold clumps. Grown with hostas and brunnera it brightened the shaded areas of the garden for several weeks each spring. Another long-flowering spurge is *E. amygdaloides robbiae* with dark evergreen leaves and delicate green 'flowers'. Mrs Fish wrote of it, 'I can forgive its running roots for its architectural beauty.' She made the most of its wandering habit by finding room for it in the ditch garden where it was allowed to make a miniature forest beneath the willows. She could always find the right place for *E. polychroma*, which makes a sunny, yellow-green dome in March: 'the embodiment of spring'. The only draw-back of this euphorbia was that it increased slowly and refused to produce seed for her. *E. polychroma* 'Major' (syn. *E. pilosa* 'Major') is a similar plant, but has the advantage of taking on rich autumn tints. Mrs Fish found it associated well with *Lobelia fulgens* or *Veronica gentianoides*. *E. polychroma* and another low-growing spurge, *E. cyparissias* (ploughman's mignonette), were quite often grown in cottage gardens. Although *E. cyparissias* is an industrious spreader, Mrs Fish liked to use it as ground cover under trees with violets and variegated periwinkle. *E. dulcis*, an inveterate seeder, was welcomed for its bright autumn colouring as was the similar, but taller, *E. coralloides* that was grown beneath a weeping silver pear alongside *Acanthus mollis* and *Polygonum cuspidatum*. When judging at a flower show, Mrs Fish was so impressed by the neat glaucous foliage of *E. portlandica* that she subsequently went to Portland Bill in Dorset to collect seed for herself. Easily mistaken for a sedum because of its fleshy leaves, *E. myrsinites* has greeny-yellow starry flowers and bracts; it looks very effective at the front of a bed or in a dry stone wall. Although many euphorbias are happy in any site, *E. myrsinites* and the larger and more erect *E. rigida*, need a warm position. Mrs Fish grew the latter with *Bergenia* × *schmidtii*, crocosmias, agapanthus and nerines on a steep, sunny bank beside the Lido. No doubt Mrs Fish's enthusiastic advocacy of euphorbias has helped to ensure their popularity today. She realised that they would appeal to future generations of gardeners because they are, 'suited to our present rather informal style, and are certainly labour-saving.'

If euphorbias were the most versatile foliage plants of the garden at East Lambrook, the bergenias were the most luxuriant ground cover: 'ground cover par excellence, ground cover at the rate of one leaf per foot, but they are magnificent foliage plants as well ... The more you live with them, the more beautiful they become.' Mrs Fish was influenced by Gertrude Jekyll's love of these plants and, like her, found that they were worth growing for their year-round interest. Following Miss Jekyll, she also liked their flowers – 'We collect bergenias for the beauty of their leaves, but the flowers are an added delight.' She grew them on their own against stone walls or beside paths, with plenty of room, so that their thick mat of large, rounded or spoon-shaped foliage could be seen at its best. However, she also recognised that they provided a perfect, solid background for less substantial plants. Like the hellebores, their full glory was best seen at East Lambrook during the winter and early spring. Mrs Fish liked most those with leaves that turn rich shades of crimson or purple, the colour persisting until the new leaf growth appears. *B. purpurascens*, *B. cordifolia* 'Purpurea' and *B.* 'Ballawley' have particularly good colouring, but she thought them not such useful ground cover as the green varieties because the leaves are more upright in growth. In the ditch garden, the winter-colouring bergenias were grown high on the banks so that their brilliant colour could be fully appreciated. Elsewhere, they were given many uses: to clothe an awkward corner, to contrast with the trailing stems of variegated blackberries, or *Lamium galeobdolon* 'Variegatum', or the plumes of pink pampas grass. They also gave substance to the skeletal silhouettes of herbaceous and silver plants that were left untrimmed throughout the winter.

The late spring is one of the most exciting times in any garden. Like all gardeners, Mrs Fish looked forward to this season with keen anticipation, but never without trepidation as she awaited signs of growth of her newest or rarest treasures: 'If gardening doesn't teach us anything else it should teach us faith.' On the banks of the ditch garden, the later primroses, chionodoxas, scillas, and erythroniums now shared the scene with a mass of new spring leaves. The emerging greenery may have been the young growth of comfrey and euphorbias or the unfurling leaves of tellima, geranium and hosta. To Mrs Fish the young, pale yellow leaves edged with pale green of *Hosta fortunei* 'Albopicta' were among the most beautiful sights in the May garden. Now was the time that they, along with hardy ferns or the lovely marbled-leaved arum, *Arum italicum marmoratum* (syn. *A. i. pictum*) became interspersed with self-seeded flowers. Many of these were allowed to remain because in Mrs Fish's philosophy, 'no garden would be complete without some of the artless little annual flowers, certainly not a garden where chance seedlings are allowed to stay and flower in the spots they have chosen for themselves.' The Welsh poppies (*Meconopsis cambrica*) that put themselves about were a mixed blessing because Mrs Fish was trying to establish the double form but, nevertheless, she still liked the single: 'it is quite irresponsible and yet it has great grace and beauty.' Also, she really wanted only the perennial *Myosotis alpestris*, but wild forget-me-nots inevitably found their way into the garden and, try as she might to hate them, she had to admit that they were 'so beautiful that I forget I am having a private war with those innocent-eyed spreaders.' Mrs Fish planted many pulmonarias in the ditch garden and spring was the time when they looked their best. She did not shun the simple cottage garden *Pulmonaria officinalis*, but also sought out rarer and more interesting varieties: 'Collecting good forms is a regular gardening sport.' Her favourites were *P. rubra* 'Bowles' Red' which had good flowers, but no silver marking on the leaves, and *P. saccharata argentea*, virtually all silver. Today there is a fine pulmonaria, *P. vallarsae* 'Margery Fish', named in tribute to her and for the work she did in popularising this group.

Trilliums raised their mottled heads above a carpet of *Mitella breweri* and the stately veratrum triplets (*V. nigrum*, *V. album* and *V. viride*), unfurled their massive, handsomely ribbed leaves. Mrs Fish grew the giant form of Solomon's seal, *Polygonatum biflorum*, the variegated form, *P. × hybridum* 'Variegatum', libertias with their white saucer-like flowers, bronze-leaved *Crocosmia* 'Solfaterre' and double camassias at the top of the bank so the flowers could be admired from below: 'The plants that hang their heads on arching stalks get the highest places so that one gets the full beauty of the plants as a whole.' Although she did not think it as lovely as the single forms, she grew the double Solomon's Seal, *P. × hybridum* 'Flore Pleno' because it was unusual. She wrote, 'I wonder why we fuss about double flowers because on the whole I don't think they compare with the single-flowered forms. But many of them have the charm of the unusual.' Several of the double flowers she did think worth growing had a home in the ditch garden. Among them was the veteran buttercup – *Ranunculus aconitifolius* 'Flore Pleno' (fair maids of Kent). It is perhaps the best of the group with its clumps of deeply-cut foliage and densely double white button flowers, but 'scarce and expensive' as Mrs Fish said. Another member of the buttercup family in the ditch garden was *Caltha palustris* 'Flore Pleno' – a most striking spring plant with its glossy leaves and golden flowers. Seedlings of lady's smock, *Cardamine pratensis* 'Flore Pleno', proliferated here, and Mrs Fish tried to distinguish these from the unwanted commoners.

Fritillaries were enjoying renewed popularity by the mid-1960s and, for some time, Mrs Fish had been collecting as many as she could buy. The dainty, named varieties like the pale lavender and white *F. meleagris* 'Poseidon', were given special treatment in troughs and raised beds but the more robust types were grown in the ditch garden. The species, *F. meleagris* was massed under old apple trees and the variegated sycamore where it grew with other spring bulbs: crocus, aconites, jonquils, grape hyacinths and narcissi. *Erythronium dens-canis* also grew here but, like the fritillaries, did not multiply. Mrs Fish did not risk growing the rarer members of the genus in grass: *E. californicum* and *E. tuolumnense*, among others, were grown in shaded, raised beds.

Irises also brought variety to the spring garden. In fact, there were irises for every season and every situation. The earliest, *I. pumila*, a dwarf bearded iris, appeared all over the garden in early April. Soon it was joined by the small bulbous species Juno irises, like *I. bucharica*, with its satiny yellow and white flowers; the rare *I. graeberiana*, with pale blue flowers; and the sturdier *I. magnifica*, with blue and white flowers. Mrs Fish thought that the lovely mourning iris, *I. susiana*, which flowered in May and June, was 'a strapping wench' compared with the other early irises.

Two charmers of the spring garden for which Mrs Fish had great affection were *Omphalodes verna* (blue-eyed Mary) and *O. cappadocica* (blue-eyed Betty). 'Betty' has tidier growth than 'Mary' and its bright blue flowers go on for many weeks. Mrs Fish asked, 'Why is it, I wonder, that blue flowers give such a feeling of innocence and simplicity?' Perhaps it is because they add a touch of coolness to the predominance of warm yellows that inhabit every garden each spring. One of the most typical spring plants of the cottager's garden was the perennial wall flower, *Cheiranthus cheiri*. Mrs Fish grew several varieties, among them 'Harpur Crewe' and the older 'Bloody Warrior.' In Mrs Fish's time, this was called 'Old Bloody Warrior.' Finding them difficult to propagate and grow, she was moved to write of the latter, 'I sometimes feel like reversing the first two words!' The star of Bethlehem, *Ornithogalum umbellatum*, another veteran plant of the cottage garden, with attractive green and white flowers, was never so difficult, but Mrs Fish was always relieved to see its flowers appearing in late May. She found it useful for naturalising in grass or in crowded shady corners. One of its less familiar relatives, *Ornithogalum nutans* was always a favourite with visitors to the garden. Mrs Fish loved it too, describing its hyacinth-like flowers in lyrical terms – 'a translucent grey that reminds me of supple grey satin.'

As April turned to May, aquilegias began to add their bonnet-like flowers to the picture: 'No cottage garden would be complete without columbines.' She preferred the short-spurred varieties to the brasher hybrids. *A. vulgaris* 'Munstead White' was one of her favourites, but not such a generous seeder as some of the others. Being somewhat hyperactive, *A.* 'Hensol Harebell' was given a border to itself: 'it is so lovely that I am grateful for its sea of blue.' Another delight of spring is the Virginian cowslip, *Mertensia virginica*, with smooth blue-grey leaves and pure blue hanging flowers – a lovely counterpart to *Lathyrus vernus alboroseus*, her favourite perennial pea. She grew several members of this group including the common perennial pea of cottage gardens, *Lathyrus latifolius*. It did well in the shade where 'the tangle of green merges pleasantly with the other plants growing up the walls.'

As the harsh weather of winter and early spring receded, the garden changed dramatically. The clearly defined evergreens, both shrubs and ground cover plants, that characterised the scene in the coldest months of the year, were swamped by an explosion of new green leaves and colour from hundreds of flowers coming into bloom. In the early months of the year, it was the ditch garden that featured most, but now the emphasis moved to all the other areas. Herbaceous plants spread themselves in every direction in the terrace garden, the rockeries overflowed with trailing plants, carpeters softened the paths and paving and climbers covered the walls, giving the garden an ethereal quality where all hard outlines were blurred. The individual plants were no less valued than when there was not so much to take the eye, but now, as well as a singular contribution, they had to fit into the emerging summer tapestry, just as they would have done in an old cottage garden.

6

The Mature Garden in Summer

'In my idea of a perfect garden there must always be something to catch the eye and keep up interest, and for this we need the handmaidens as well as the stars.'

As SUMMER APPROACHED, it was the profusion of cottage garden plants that gave the garden its characteristic uncontrived appearance, but it was the way in which Mrs Fish mixed these with more rarified plants that gave the garden special distinction. Like other cottage gardeners she allowed her plants to intermingle at will, often finding that they accidentally arranged themselves in pleasing associations but she always kept a watchful eye to ensure that the harmonious balance was not lost. Her preference was for soft colours, but inevitably brighter ones crept in.

Apart from the choice of plants and their arrangement, the way in which they were grown was essential to the East Lambrook style. Although Mrs Fish's aim was to grow only those plants that did not require staking, inevitably there were some by which she was seduced that needed support: 'June is the time when one discovers if one has planted too closely, and I always have, and if one has staked sufficiently and efficiently, and I never have.' She used iron half-hoops to support a few plants such as the taller asters and chrysanthemums, but tried to place most of her lankier plants where their limbs could be contained. She put them in a corner, against a wall, supported them by sturdier perennials or encouraged them to grow through shrubs. She cut back

Michaelmas daisies, golden rod and heleniums early in the season so that they made only half their natural height and would flower later.

As plants that adapted their habit of growth to their neighbours Mrs Fish found the herbaceous potentillas indispensable. With tall perennials, they assume an upright habit but if given room to spread, can cover a large area; they are good disguisers and make excellent ground cover: 'I like the way they go on blooming for several months, and their obliging habit of fitting their ways to mine.' When the poppies' dying foliage had to be cut back in late June, potentillas usefully filled the gaps. *P.* 'Etna', a single maroon, was one Mrs Fish used in this way, as were the pink *P.* 'Miss Willmott' and *P.* 'Gibson's Scarlet'. The primrose-yellow *P. recta pallida* seeded itself here and there and its loose growth needed restraining. It was tied to a shrubby *Prunus × subhirtella* 'Autumnalis' and encouraged to weave through *Philadelphus* 'Beauclerk'.

In the profusion of summer growth Mrs Fish valued foliage of emphatic shape like the blade-like leaves of irises: 'I would always find room for a few, whatever the size of my garden, because they can be grown in narrow beds and odd corners and the foliage is beautiful throughout the year.' For early summer she had *Iris pallida* 'Aurea Variegata' and *I. p.* 'Argentea Variegata' – 'so lovely and so very slow to increase.' Adding sparkle to the green of early summer was *I. setosa* in rich purple, blotched white and veined yellow. In the ditch garden were forms of the fast-increasing *I. sibirica* – the varieties 'Snow Queen' and 'Eric the Red' were her favourites. Following them came *I. orientalis*, an old garden favourite in white and yellow: 'Nothing could be more stately than a good clump of this species.' The clumps in the ditch garden made fine companions for the hostas grown around their feet.

As the garden developed, the bold structural foliage of hostas became an integral part of the scene: 'Quite unhesitatingly, I put the hostas among the most accommodating and – to me – the most beautiful members of the whole lily family of plants. They have few foibles about soil and position and are practically inde-structible.' In the early 1960s, hosta hybridising in America and Japan aroused great interest and, with her intuitive sense of plants with a future, as well as those with a past, Mrs Fish was devoted to them. In fact she had bought two of her favourites in America long before they became available in Britain – *H. lancifolia* and *H. sieboldiana elegans*. But 'for sheer beauty the great crinkled leaves of *Hosta sieboldiana* come first.' She found the large-leaved hostas offered luxuriant summer cover for shaded parts of the garden, between shrubs or as companions for border perennials. Those with margined or splashed leaves looked best in darker shade where their white, lime green or gold variegations showed up more emphatically. Mrs Fish was as easily seduced by new arrivals as she was by old garden favourites. So long as a plant could contribute to the overall picture in her garden, she could be tempted.

Erigerons were one of the temptations: 'I like the new erigerons with their big flowers in exciting new colours, but they haven't the long-flowering qualities of some of the old ones.' Although she was seduced by the modern varieties, Mrs Fish still preferred the veterans like *E. philadelphicus* which she massed to show their small pink daisies to better effect. Other favourites were *E. speciosus macranthus* (syn. *E. mesa-grande*), welcome for its succession of pleasing lavender flowers, and the delicately-flowered *E.* 'Quakeress', one of the cottage garden daisies, which she grew in association with the pale blue form of *Viola cornuta*. Although it needed support for its flaying arms, Mrs Fish described *E. multiradiatus*, as 'one of the toughest and most good-tempered plants I know' – and she knew it well, having had it since she started gardening. She called another old friend, *E. glaucus*, 'my unruly daisy', but found its greyish-green leaves topped with mauve flowers useful as ground cover.

The *Bellis* genus are daisies of a smaller and more disciplined kind and 'No self-respecting cottage garden would be without its little edging of daisies.' One of the best is *B. perennis* 'Dresden China'. Mrs Fish originally grew it in paving crevices or at the edge of paths, but subsequently found that it was happiest in the light shade of shrubs and perennials. *B.* 'Rob Roy', with big crimson flowers on long stalks, was used in her terrace borders against the paths while *B.* 'Prolifera', 'Hen-and-Chicken', which likes a rich, moist run, regular division and top-dressing, was very happy when shaded by rosemary and *Buddleja alternifolia* in the centre of one of the beds. These little flowers never lost their charm for Mrs Fish: 'All these daisies are easy to grow and all have that sign of good breeding and are at home in any society.'

The cottagers valued any plant with a long flowering season. The daisies flower for a long time as does catmint, one of the plants most firmly associated with a cottage garden. The cottagers' plant, *Nepeta × faassenii*, was considered by Mrs Fish to be the best of the genus for most purposes, but she thought it was a waste of space to use it in a border where invariably it takes up too much room. She preferred to see it growing on top, in, or at the bottom of a wall or beside a path where its grey foliage and mist of lavender flowers would soften the hardness of the stone. It is also a good ground cover for inaccessible places because it needs so little attention. She also grew the variety 'Six Hills Giant', a much larger cousin, which went perfectly with the pale pink flowers of *Erigeron* 'Charity' and the rugosa rose 'Roseraie de l'Haÿ'. The beguilingly-named *Nepeta* 'Souvenir d'André Chaudron', with grey-blue flowers, was used to cool down the strident magenta of *Lychnis viscaria* 'Splendens Plena'. A less commonly grown member of the group is *N. nervosa* with fluffy blue flower spikes and distinctively-veined leaves. As it wanders somewhat, Mrs Fish contained this lovely plant in a stone crevice or narrow border.

'Peonies grow in popularity every year because they are perfect for our present style of gardening ... Nothing could be better for growing among shrubs and in other permanent plantings.' Mrs Fish was always aware of the virtues of good plants that did not need laborious attention, recognising that not everyone was as dedicated a gardener as she was. Peonies are the kind of plant that she thought should be used more in modern gardens. Not only are the flowers beautiful but the foliage keeps its sheen for a long time through the summer and makes a valuable foil for other flowers when its own flowering period is over. In the autumn many have leaves that turn a brilliant colour and some like *P. mlokosewitschii* have wonderful seedpods with silky insides. At East Lambrook the earliest peony, *P. tenuifolia*, came into flower in April. This, an ancient cottage plant, was given to her in 1940 when she was still a novice gardener and she planted it on the top level of one of the rockeries, an unusual site that apparently suited it well as it rewarded her by spreading slowly and flowering regularly. The double red cottage peony *P. officinalis* 'Rubra

Plena' was, however, not one that she considered appropriate for a border. Like her mentor, William Robinson, she thought its best use was in the wild garden among shrubs. To her taste, its foliage was too heavy for its flowers. But she recalled a cottage in a nearby village where it gave her great pleasure, growing on either side of the front door and flowering for at least a month. Her quibble with some peonies, the modern hybrids in particular, was that they have a very short flowering period and in general she preferred the species and their forms. Not all species, however, have long flowering periods. The magnificent single yellow *P. mlokosewitschii* flowers only briefly. Mrs Fish grew it and admired the elegance of its delicate flowers, the autumn colour of its leaves and the cherry colour of the inside of its seed pods which highlight its shiny black seeds. Another member of the genus of which she thought highly was *P. cambessedesii*, a native of the Balearic Isles. It was grown in a bed near the house with other items that needed to be nursed, like her precious double sweet rocket (*Hesperis matronalis* double form). A peony that has the most dazzling blood red single flowers, *P. peregrina*, Mrs Fish grew in both sun and shade, but for her its colour was more intense when seen in light shade.

A characteristic cottage garden plant is Jacob's ladder, *Polemonium caeruleum*. It was not a favourite of Mrs Fish's and she preferred some of the more unusual species and the modern hybrids. She thought the old Jacob's ladder was probably best grown in woodland with pulmonarias, bugles and some of the more rampant geraniums. For her borders she preferred to have the improved version *P. × richardsonii* which has bigger flower spikes whose florets all open at the same time. The pink *P. carneum* appealed to her because it seemed more informal and graceful than the blue types and she liked to see it growing under a bush of double coral-flowered chaenomeles with a group of off-white tulips nearby. When one of her polemoniums produced unusual offspring, Mrs Fish called them *P. reptans* 'Lambrook Manor'. They were taller than the type and had a longer flowering season and so were good subjects for growing among larger perennials. For the same reason, she liked *P. foliosissimum*; it has the added bonus of staying in flower until November. She thought the richer colour of *P. reptans* 'Sapphire' was useful because it gave substance to the rather flimsy growth of *Erigeron philadelphicus*.

The polemoniums fitted into any garden scene but sometimes the more pushy members of the family elbowed their way in where they were not wanted. The same thing happened with the lychnis tribe, particularly *L. flos-jovis*. Other lychnis also had the disadvantage of being difficult to place because of their colour – *L. chalcedonica*, for instance, with its strident orange-red flowers, and *L. viscaria* 'Splendens Plena' with even brighter ones. However, Mrs Fish thought the latter was tolerable in the company of nepetas or lavender-blue *Scutellaria incana*. Not all lychnis are so difficult to place. Some make handsome silver rosettes in the winter and have easier colours – *L. coronaria* with magenta flowers, *L.* × *walkeri* 'Abbotswood Rose', with velvet red flowers and *L. flos-jovis*, with candy-pink flowers – a colour much loved by Mrs Fish. A close relative of the lychnis, *Silene dioica* 'Rosea Plena', the double red campion, was grown by Mrs Fish, even though it could easily be mistaken for a weed when young.

Mrs Fish tolerated some invasive plants that would have been grubbed out by those wanting a more ordered appearance. Her ideal of the wild garden did not call for strict control. Of course, there were some things that she just did not want in her garden and others that started off as being welcome guests, only to prove nuisances in time. When first given *Veronica filiformis*, she admired its sheets of green and vivid blue flowers. However, when it became apparent how invasive it is, she worked hard to get rid of it. The ordinary bugle was also officially banished, but still maintained a foothold. *Ajuga pyramidalis* and *A. reptans* 'Multicolor' had better manners and associated well with gold and silver plants and glaucous foliage and became respected members of the community. Of the incomparably ill-mannered soapwort, *Saponaria officinalis* 'Rosea Plena' (bouncing Bet) Mrs Fish complained, 'I am still waging war on this lady.' However, she found a welcome home for her and the dreaded *Cerastium tomentosum* at Brympton d'Evercy where Mrs Clive had room to accommodate them in her grand schemes. If people arrived with empty baskets to be filled with plants for their new and naked gardens, Mrs Fish would fill them with the orange-flowered hawkweed *Hieracium aurantiacum*, certain to cover any empty space. *Campanula glomerata* was no less invasive but Mrs Fish liked its rich purplish-blue flowers that appeared at a time in summer when they were most needed. Her advice about these over-enthusiastic characters was to give them less than ideal growing conditions in the hope that this would restrain them. There were, of course, more obliging fillers and carpeters to be seen in the summer garden at East Lambrook. *Filipendula vulgaris* and the even more handsome *F. palmata*, were used to clothe the odd patch with their thick, ferny foliage; the soft silky grey-green *Ballota pseudodictamnus* was allowed to fall over low walls onto paths; the ornamental strawberries *Fragaria vesca monophylla* and *F. v.* 'Plymouth Strawberry' were given space to wander beneath shrubs and perennials while their smaller relations, *F. vesca semperflorens* (syn. *F. alpina*) and *F.* 'Baron Solemacher', were used as edging plants. Prunellas, planted around the garden, made good carpeters and adapted to sun or shade. *P.* 'Loveliness' makes a particularly attractive effect of dark green foliage and pale blue flowers.

As the garden matured, an army of creepers, carpeters and smotherers took possession of the lower ground. They crept across the stone terraces, filled crevices in the walls and paving and softened edges of paths. Plants like dwarf phlox, little irises and sisyrinchiums grew in cracks in the stone, while the old dependables – thrift, alpine strawberries and rock campanulas, *C. portenschlagiana* and *C. poscharskyana*, looked most effective growing in dry stone walls. In the low wall that separated the lawn from the drive, bushy thymes, silver-leaved dianthus, campanulas and *Geranium sanguineum striatum* made a mat of pastel shades. *Ajuga pyramidalis* sat on a sea of blue-grey *Acaena buchananii* and bronze and crimson *A. microphylla*. Dwarf variegated grasses, clumps of lady's mantle (*Alchemilla mollis*) and E. A. Bowles's beetroot-leaved plantain grew at the path's edge. Thymes, mints, acaenas and mossy saxifrages made harlequin patterns over the paving and paths with the more robust creepers and carpeters at the front of borders.

Saxifraga × *urbium* (London pride) and *Stachys byzantina* (lamb's ears) were among the plants used in this way. Although they are very common today, until the early 1960s neither of these plants was widely used in the average garden. Mrs Fish recommended London pride not only for edging, but also for growing in and under walls and as ground cover. She thought the soft, woolly foliage of lamb's ears, with its flowers removed, made an effective underplanting for roses. In the early 1960s she was one of the first gardeners to use the recently discovered *Stachys byzantina* 'Silver

Carpet' (syn. *S. lanata* 'Silver Carpet'), a valuable non-flowering cultivar.

Pinks, those other valuable finishers to the edge of a bed or side of a path, always enchanted Mrs Fish. She valued their old-fashioned flowers, their fragrance and their silvery-green foliage: 'Whenever we think of an old world garden we think of pinks, Gillyflowers they were called in the old days, or Sweet Johns, and they belong, more than any other flower, to the days of sun bonnets and print gowns and the little crowded gardens of the past.' Although she admired the haphazard way the cottagers grew their pinks, in her own garden she generally adopted a more modern approach. Certainly, she grew some old laced pinks as an edging to paths in the traditional way, where their scent could be appreciated, but she grew most of the others as ground cover. Those with glaucous foliage were particularly effective, and among the varieties she suggested were the Highland hybrids and 'Thomas'. One of her favourite pinks was the single 'Brympton Red', originally given to her by Mrs Clive, which is useful for growing in any position.

Mrs Fish loved the unassuming beauty of hedgerow plants: 'One of the joys of the countryside in summer is the white froth of cow parsley in the hedgerows.' None was too commonplace to comment on and some were even considered worthy of intro-duction into the garden. Sweet woodruff (*Galium odoratum*) for example 'The scent of new-mown hay is delicious and its dainty elegance is a good background for more stolid plants.' While she would never let wild cow parsley into the garden, she did have two of its more domestic relations because they made good foil plants: Cambridge parsley (*Selinum tenuifolium*) in the ditch garden and the pink cow parsley (*Pimpinella major rosea*) in the terrace garden. She described the pimpinella's faded pink flowers as having an 'old-world dowdiness' and liked it under a Judas tree (*Cercis siliquastrum*) with *Campanula glomerata*, and elsewhere with Jacob's ladder and the grass *Phalaris arundinacea* 'Aureovariegata' with a blue cedar as a background. Thrift, *Armeria maritima*, was another native plant that Mrs Fish thought merited inclusion as an edging. She grew the deep pink variety, *A. m.* 'Bee's Ruby' in stone paving and in narrow beds where its outline could be seen and the white form, *A. m.* 'Alba', among the stones around the barton's grass circle.

There was nothing 'common' about many of the self-seeders that contributed so much to the garden's informal spirit. These opportunists were often allowed to stay in their chosen abode, or, if time allowed, Mrs Fish would collect their seedlings and plant them in groups to make a stronger emphasis. *Gladiolus communis byzantinus* is a profligate seeder whose progeny she gathered together and placed in the paved front garden next to the grey-leaved *Teucrium fruticans*. Other seedlings of this gladiolus appeared below a *Ceanothus* × *veitchianus* while more were encouraged to grow among variegated honesty. Although the seedlings could become a nuisance she always admired their flower form: 'Each flower is a picture, for the soft magenta petals have the iridescence one finds in begonias.'

Some of her favourite seeders in the garden were the various kinds of onion (*Allium*) and their close relations: 'I wouldn't be without the good tempered *Allium moly*, with its globes of yellow star-like flowers and good seed-heads.' She much admired *Nectaroscordum siculum*, that most elegant of the onion tribe, with green and cream bells whose insides are decorated with maroon markings: 'This is a plant that is gaining favour and I think will soon be found in many catalogues.' She considered *Allium roseum* a little too generous in its seeding and preferred to grow the larger varieties that did well in her clay soil like *A. christophii*, *A. sphaerocephalon*, and *A. rosenbachianum*.

The astrantias (Hattie's pincushion, or melancholy gentleman) have also been found in cottage gardens for a long time, but had only recently come to be valued by all kinds of gardener: 'The present interest in astrantias is just another example of the uncanny way the cottagers had of finding and keeping a good plant.' As the garden at East Lambrook developed, astrantias were among its most distinctive and versatile features: 'They fit in so well with our informal mixed borders and are the perfect plants to grow with shrubs; they are, in fact, the best of good mixers.' Their flowers, composed of florets and bracts in variations of delicate cream, green and pink, fascinated her: 'They are not melancholy to me, not even sombre, merely delicate in construction and colour, with a fine upright habit and always smiling faces.' She also wrote: 'A good show of colour used to be the criterion of a good garden but nowadays the flowers that raise the most enthusiasm are not always the most colourful ones.

Shape, texture and the right setting are often more important considerations.' *Astrantia maxima*, with muted pink centres, surrounded by pale green bracts, was the one she liked best, not only for its flowers, but also for its three-lobed leaves that resemble a young hellebore's; its old name was 'helleborifolia' and Mrs Fish could not understand why it was ever changed to the less descriptive 'maxima'. There were many clumps of *A. major* in the garden. This astrantia, with green and white flowers, is larger than 'maxima' and seeds prolifically. Mrs Fish also grew *A. carniolica*, the whitest of the species, and *A. c. rubra*, that has dusty crimson flowers. The latter made a pretty picture grown with the palest pink *Dianthus gratianopolitanus* and *D. g.* 'Double Cheddar'. Mrs Fish decided that 'major' and 'carniolica' were so alike that it was pointless separating them. In her books she writes about an unusual form of *A. major* that arose in cottage gardens in Gloucestershire. It has very long and shaggy bracts and grows to about 3 feet. She could find no name for it, so when she gave plants to other gardeners, it became known as *A. major* 'Shaggy'.

No account of Mrs Fish's summer garden would be adequate without a description of her geraniums which she regarded as essential in any garden. As she collected more and more, their refined flowers and finely-cut foliage found their way into every area of East Lambrook. The more rampant of them, however, were banished to the orchard and the ditch garden, whereas those with more distinction and restraint were given homes in the terrace garden and the rockeries. It was a problem to find the best site for some of them: 'With such excellent shade plants as geraniums, it is not always easy to decide which are the purely woodland types and which are suitable for the more formal planting in a border.' To start with she kept all the varieties of *Geranium pratense* in the wilder parts of the garden, 'because in my mind they belong to the hedgerows – it is to the wild they belong.' However, she changed her mind after seeing the double purple geranium (*G. pratense* 'Plenum Violaceum') treated with greater respect in the violet border at Sissinghurst. She then went on to plant the double white, blue and purple pratense types in her terrace beds. Unfortunately, Mrs Fish never had enough space to accommodate the quantities of informal and rampant geraniums she would have liked. Among those she did find room for were the pink flowered, crimson veined *G. pratense* 'Striatum', the taller pinkish-purple flowered *G. sylvaticum*, and *G. viscosissimum*, 3-feet tall with veined pink flowers. Of the taller types, the only one she liked in the border was *G. psilostemon*: 'I love it at every stage of the game. Those black-centred crude magenta flowers would be sinister if they did not grow gracefully above the most elegant cut foliage, rich in autumn tints.' She thought this geranium associated well with the moss rose 'William Lobb.' *G. delavayi* was one whose position she changed her mind about; at first she grew it in a shady corner, but after seeing it in a border at the Savill Gardens, moved it to a more prominent position. The way Colonel Savill used it made her look again at its beautifully marked leaves and reflexed crimson flowers. She had some doubts about the tall *G. ibericum*, believing that it looked right in a more unkempt cottage garden but not in her own, 'I love it dearly when it is a sheet of blue and wonder why we don't use more of it.' It was not used in her borders because it gets so untidy after flowering and therefore was grown among shrubs and in the orchard. At one time, however, she grew the closely related *G.* x *magnificum* (syn. *G. ibericum platypetalum*) as ground cover under *Magnolia grandiflora* 'Exmouth': 'The geranium has made a sea of tossing dark leaves under the richness of bronze and glistening green and is a lovely sight when covered with large violet-purple flowers in June.' There is one tall geranium that she felt was better grown as a specimen rather than in a bed or wild area; *G. palmatum*, a tender species with striking deeply-cut foliage, seemed perfectly suited for growing in a pot in a courtyard where its glossy foliage can be seen best.

One of the smaller geraniums she did like to see in the terrace beds was *G. himalayense* 'Gravetye'. This geranium, with blue flowers marked with a reddish centre, has the advantage of not minding sun or shade and blooms over a long period. She grew it around a crab-apple tree where it looked especially good when the tree was bare. This was one geranium she thought could be planted in a formal border in front of shrubs where it would 'merge formality happily with informality.' One of her great favourites was *G. endressii*: 'I would not be without *G. endressii*, with its pink flowers and soft grey leaves.' When she first made the terrace garden she used *G. e.* 'Wargrave Pink' to provide colour and ground cover near her 'pudding' trees and on the steep bank above the Lido. From these sites it seeded itself throughout the garden, coming out from under trees and even in cracks in the paving: 'It is the easiest plant to increase or decrease, and is always a lady.' Other geraniums that she considered to be excellent ground cover are *G. phaeum album*, 'it is quite a pleasant little soul'; *G. macrorrhizum*, 'I like the rosey-purple of its flowers'; and *G. m. album*, 'my favourite for all purposes.' The macrorrhizum types she grew for their scented and autumn-colouring foliage but consigned them to wilder areas.

The geraniums with small flowers but well-marked leaves looked good under old and species roses. She suggested *G. nodosum*, *G. phaeum* and the taller *G. reflexum*, although again, they were not generally suitable for formal planting. She thought the grey-green evergreen leaves of *G. renardii* were 'an acquisition anywhere' and liked to see them against red or dark-leaved plants. She did not allow it to get too big because it flowers better if restricted. The dwarf *G. malviflorum* was welcome for its fresh fern-like foliage in autumn and its blue flowers veined with red. She also admired several varieties of *G. × oxonianum*; 'Claridge Druce' grows well in shade and has beautiful foliage; 'Rose Clair' with its purple-veined white flowers is perfectly suited to a woodland site; and 'A. T. Johnson' has small dancing flowers that 'are a delicious shade of silvery-pink.' Mrs Fish had mixed feelings about *G. sanguineum*: 'Sometimes I am very mean to the good-tempered "Bloody Cranesbill".' She pulled it out in armfuls because it ran too much, but conceded that in the right place this low-growing geranium with crimson-magenta flowers had its uses. At other times she thought it deserved its name when it trespassed on other plants and made walls disintegrate. She much preferred the variety *G. s. striatum*: 'she is a perfect lady, and you find her in the most exclusive rock gardens.' Among others that were grown in her rock garden were the trailing *G. × riversleaianum* 'Russell Prichard' and *G. wallichianum* 'Buxton's Variety'. She thought the latter's beautifully-shaped leaves and powder-blue and white flowers were among 'one of the joys of autumn', and it was excellent for smothering odd corners and the bare ground between shrubs. As with other plant groups Mrs Fish studied their form and habits minutely and was therefore able to use them effectively in different situations.

Campanulas were another group of special importance: 'No family gives us more ideas for the shady border than the campanulas.' There was, for her, a campanula to suit every situation. Her introduction to them was through the old cottage favourite, *Campanula latiloba*, a tall plant with white or blue flowers that was an inhabitant of the cottager's crowded border. However, Mrs Fish did not grow it in the traditional manner; for her its rampant ways and tolerance of poor soil, made it more suitable for planting under trees and conifers. One campanula that was found in the borders was the peach-leaved bell flower, *C. persicifolia* – 'Among the daintiest flowers we grow.' As well as having beautiful blue or white flowers, this evergreen plant had a knack of seeding itself obligingly in just the right place at the edge of a path or beneath a wall. Once again, she preferred the species and their forms to the hybrids, and she grew every white form she could: 'The pure white form of *C. persicifolia alba* is one of the loveliest flowers in the garden.' The stouter *C. lactiflora* with its sprays of milky blue flowers, proved to be a good mixer in the terrace beds or wilder parts of the garden, and if cut back after its first flowering, gave a second flush in late summer. Another campanula that will respond to this treatment is *C. alliariifolia*. With its clumps of heart-shaped leaves and wiry stems of white bells, Mrs Fish found it most effective in a narrow border. Most of the campanulas enjoy a shaded home and *C. latifolia macrantha* was placed under the architectural foliage of *Angelica archangelica*.

Campanulas were a subject that Mrs Fish returned to again and again in her writing and lectures, treating them with a familiarity born of long friendship. Of *C.* 'Burghaltii' – one of only a few hybrids in the garden – she wrote: 'One of those comfortable plants that give no trouble and are always pleasant to meet.' She described the delicate pink *C. latifolia* 'Loddon Anna', as 'particularly charming'. However, she did not feel equally friendly to all the family. The rock campanula, *C. poscharskyana* was not so well behaved as some: 'sometimes I wish I had never introduced this rampant campanula to the garden.' Of the rock species, she particularly liked *C. carpatica* and its varieties in violet blue and white, perhaps because as a new gardener, she had used it to cover her dry stone walls. Although she had a sentimental attachment to this campanula, her favourites of all the smaller species were *C. persicifolia planiflora alba*, that makes neat green rosettes below short spikes of white flowers, and *C. p. p.* 'Coronata' in blue. Mrs Fish grew both these in her rock garden, along with *C. isophylla*, which thrived in the shade of a spurge that hung over the wall.

'I am always preaching penstemon for continuous colour in the summer garden': their long flowering period from June until late autumn and unfussiness as to soil or position made them valuable for mixing with other plants in her long border and the terrace beds. Of the softer coloured members of this family, she loved the small shell-pink flowers of *Penstemon* 'Hewell's Pink' and the opal-blue of *P.* 'Stapleford Gem'. The latter looked very pretty against the bronze foliage and cherry-red flowers of the 'Rosemary Rose' with smouldering bronze fennel alongside. *P.* 'Alice Hindley', another good blue of sturdy growth, was 'a rangy thoroughbred, a shootin', huntin' and fishin' woman, who is elegant in a raw-boned way.' Tall *P.* 'Pennington Gem' in soft pink, needed to be discreetly staked, but E. A. Bowles's little *P.* 'Myddelton Gem' fitted tidily into any corner. Bolder red varieties gave dabs of brilliant colour among perennials of muted colour: *P.* 'George Home', originally from Hidcote, has glowing red flowers and good bright foliage; *P.* 'Schönholzeri' grows neatly and has fiery-red flowers; Mrs Fish liked to see the wine-red, crimson-flushed flowers of *P.* 'Andenken an Friedrich Hahn' (syn. *P.* 'Garnet') – with the sun behind them. A tender penstemon, *P. isophyllus* with grey-green leaves and small coral flowers on tall stems, needs a sheltered site, so Mrs Fish grew it against a wall on top of the rock garden with *Senecio vira-vira*. She found that some penstemons prefer lime-free soil; for example, *P. barbatus* with scarlet, foxglove flowers on branching stems and *P. heterophyllus*, a pretty plant with bronze leaves and clear steely-blue flowers over a long season. Despite the fact that penstemons have a reputation for being not quite hardy, Mrs Fish found them 'one of the easiest subjects in the garden.'

The same was not true of some of her roses. Her heavy clay soil did not suit all those she grew, despite the fact that she treated it regularly with compost. Many kinds of roses were grown at East Lambrook from the very old Alba 'Great Maiden's Blush', found in the garden when Mrs Fish and Walter first arrived and reputed to have grown there for over one hundred years, to the newer bush roses. 'There is no flower more beautiful and satisfying than a rose, but the bushes on which they grow are bearable only when in full leaf and covered in flowers.' She disliked the practice of growing them in formal rose gardens or on their own with a carpet underplanting. She thought they should be grown as in a cottage garden – in mixed borders or singly at the back of a bed or against a wall with other climbers: 'I do not treat my roses like sacred cows but regard them as ordinary plants used to beautify the garden.' While she loved the old varieties grown by the cottagers, she also experimented with the newer Hybrid Teas and Floribundas. Often, she grew several of one variety together in a border to produce a greater impact, carefully selecting suitable companions for them. For example, in one bed she placed a group of the dark crimson Floribunda 'Frensham' among clumps of soft blue Michaelmas daisies while elsewhere she grew them with the tall spires of *Salvia sclarea turkestanica*; the shrub rose 'Magenta' was underplanted with purple sage and a group of the Hybrid Tea 'Sterling Silver', with elegant mauve flowers, was planted with *Achillea millefolium* 'Cerise Queen'. The Floribunda 'Iceberg' looked best planted in groups of at least three with a froth of silvery foliage at their feet and with plants of soft yellow flowers nearby. At East Lambrook the silver foliage was provided by *Centaurea cineraria cineraria* (syn. *C. gymnocarpa*) or *Artemisia absinthium* 'Lambrook Silver' and the yellow flowers of *Iris* 'Paper Moon' and *Aconitum lycoctonum vulparia* and, later in the autumn, *Rudbeckia fulgida sullivantii* 'Goldsturm' (black-eyed Susan) and silver *Helichrysum splendidum*.

Mrs Fish discovered, like other gardeners, that some roses make excellent ground cover, but the ground must be absolutely clean. In her time there were not the purpose-bred carpet roses we have today, but that did not deter her. She recommended pegging down the long trailing stems that some roses produce, encouraging the rose to flower all along its stems. The Hybrid Perpetual roses can be treated in this way; R. 'Frau Karl Druschki', with its pure white flowers tinged pink in bud; the double pink flowered, 'Mrs John Laing' and the Dickson brothers – 'Hugh' and 'George'. A small shrub or tree like *Prunus* × *subhirtella* 'Autumnalis' or spring-flowering magnolias could be enhanced by surrounding them with roses grown in this way. Also, she thought it possible to peg the old favourites 'American Pillar' and 'Dorothy Perkins' but herself preferred to use the softer-coloured 'New Dawn', 'Alberic Barbier', 'Sanders' White Rambler' and 'Albertine', her favourite climber. There were, for her, some low-growing roses that could be used for ground cover without assistance from the gardener such as *R. wichuraiana* which grows very close to the ground and has pale cream flowers and small glossy leaves. However, there were other taller roses that she suggested also made good ground cover without pegging: 'The normal conception of ground cover is something flat and carpeting, but if I had a large space in a border which I wanted covered for permanent beauty, I would plant the rugosa rose 'Fru Dagmar Hastrup'. Others she suggested could be used in this way included *R.* 'Schneelicht', *R.* × *jacksonii* 'Max Graf' and the lovely white *R.* 'Paulii' that looks best trailing over a wall or bank. Among the roses that sprawl and, in so doing, suppress weeds, she thought *R. macrantha* and its hybrids, *R.* 'Daisy Hill' and *R.* 'Raubritter' all worthy of inclusion.

Among Mrs Fish's favourite roses were the China roses *R.* 'Mutabilis' – 'A slender graceful creature that looks well in a corner'; and *R.* 'Viridiflora' – 'It is queer ... but I enjoy its crumpled harmony of dull green and faded crimson and would always want it in the garden.' Perhaps her favourite Floribunda rose was 'Rosemary Rose', a late flowerer with an old rose scent and purple leaves that keep their colour. Another rose she considered outstanding was 'Guinée', with its dark velvety-crimson flowers and heady scent. With her mind always on keeping her garden interesting throughout the year, she appreciated those roses that flowered late and kept their flowers into the winter. Of these, she particularly liked 'Madame Abel Chatenay', wreathed around the dining-room window, 'Zéphirine Drouhin', that flowered on the barton wall at a time when, 'I thought all good roses had gone to sleep' and 'Dr van Fleet', of which she wrote, 'I am enchanted by the shell pink flowers opening against the wall, with the heavy limbs of *Garrya elliptica* making a canopy over them.' Far from being tempted to pick these late flowers and bring them into the house, Mrs Fish, displaying that streak of romanticism that rose to the surface from time to time, was adamant that their place was in the garden: 'I am never tempted to pick my late roses because I love to see them growing in the autumn mists and to smell them in the early morning, when the garden is sparkling with heavy dew, or in the dusk when the smell of late roses mingles with wet leaves.'

She was as innovative with clematis as she was with roses. Some were grown in the normal, highly-disciplined up-the-wall, over-a-trellis way, but she preferred to see them clambering into trees, invading shrubs or mingling with their neighbours in borders: 'As well as enjoying freedom of movement I think plants enjoy living with each other, and the clematis does far better when growing at close quarters with other plants.' The more vigorous types were inclined to do this without any encouragement, while others needed to be persuaded. The strong-growing semi-her-baceous *C. heracleifolia davidiana* was one she grew so that it threw its tendrils over a group of *Polygonum amplexicaule* 'Album' or the elegant *Lysimachia clethroides* and pink Japanese anemones. It was not only the semi-herbaceous types that she liked to see used in this way, but also the true climbers: 'I have often thought how much easier it would be to loosen their bonds and let those luxuriant stems tumble about together on the ground.' *C.* 'Alba Luxurians' with small white flowers tipped with green, was planted under a north wall but Mrs Fish decided that it was happier roaming over other plants instead of being trained up the wall. Similarly she found that the evergreen *C. armandii* objected to being restricted to a wall, preferring to amble among other plants. In a corner between the malthouse and cowhouse, it weaved its way through *Stauntonia hexaphylla* and over *Euphorbia lathyrus* and a tall thalictrum.

Mrs Fish called *Clematis tibetana vernayi* L S & E 13342, 'the greatest clematis discovery of recent times.' She grew one around the kitchen window and another against the eastern boundary wall behind the long border where it was allowed to tumble into the border. From June, when the flowers appeared against sea-green foliage, the waxy petals turned from green through yellow to orange, ending their season in November as silky tassels. One of her earliest buys were several plants of the carmine hybrid *C.* 'Ville de Lyon' that were planted on the top terrace of the rock garden near the garden gate. This was when Walter was still alive and, in his meticulous fashion, helped her train them: 'How lovely they look growing over a lowish wall, rather like a beautiful oriental carpet flung over the wall.' In general she found the species clematis easier to grow than the hybrids and they certainly helped furnish the walls of the outbuildings. She grew *C. rehderiana*, with its small green cow-slip scented flowers, on the east wall of the cowhouse. Here it was accompanied by *Viburnum farreri*, the single pink rose *R.* 'Complicata' and yellow *Clematis tangutica*. As the 'rehderiana' flowered later than the 'tangutica', the pale silky seed-heads of the latter were encouraged to remain, adding to the beauty of the 'rehderiana'. Another clematis that did not keep to its intended route was *C.* 'Kermesina'. Mrs Fish placed it so that its small ruby flowers would grow through a variegated privet, *Ligustrum ovalifolium* 'Argenteum', to one side of the silver pear (*Pyrus salicifolia* 'Pendula') at the top of the terrace garden. However, the clematis soon hauled itself up into the pear tree where its flowers overlooked the neighbour's garden.

Mrs Fish liked to see roses and clematis growing together and arranged some effective associations throughout the garden. She grew the deep blue *C.* 'Perle d'Azur' against one of her largest apple trees with the champagne-coloured rose 'Breeze Hill'; the rose flowered first allowing the blue of the clematis to steal the scene. Against the eastern boundary wall, she planted *C.* 'Etoile Violette', encouraging it to grow through the pale pink rose 'New Dawn' with the deeper pink flowers of *C.* 'Comtesse de Bouchaud' nearby and purple sage beneath. She made an elderly Williams pear host for *C.* 'Lady Northcliffe' with its Wedgwood blue flowers and the rose *R. filipes* 'Kiftsgate'. The rose grew vigorously, filling the pear with its scented white flowers, while the clematis kept to the lower half of the tree, displaying its flowers to perfection.

A recurrent theme at East Lambrook was the widespread use of grey and silver plants which were so versatile and effective. Here, while Mrs Fish was certainly influenced by other gardeners, she explored the uses of silver-leaved plants as never before. E. A. Bowles was a great 'silver' man who grew all his silver plants together; Miss Ellen Willmott was so captivated by the giant thistle *Eryngium giganteum* and used it so much, scattering its seeds in other people's gardens, that after her death it became known as 'Miss Willmott's Ghost'; and Miss Jekyll was well aware of their value and had made a notable grey border at Hestercombe, not far from East Lambrook.

Mrs Fish drew on their ideas, at first using her silver plants as part of planting schemes in the terrace garden and the long border. They were used to make semi-permanent features while the more colourful flowers came and went. They were 'semi-permanent' because some were cut back in the autumn, others were cut down in the spring and some were lost because they were not fully hardy. She admired the way their silver leaves brightened and lightened the summer scene, and calmed down brighter-coloured flowers in the borders. In the mid 1960s Mrs Fish made a garden entirely devoted to silver plants. She abandoned her small enclosed vegetable garden on the west side of the house and decided that its south-facing aspect and warm, dry soil were perfect for growing silver plants. This new garden with its favoured site gave her the opportunity to experiment with new and 'difficult' plants, while the less demanding ones were grown elsewhere.

In the sunnier areas she was particularly fond of artemisias. Her only reservation about them was that 'all the artemisias have to be curbed at times as they have no respect for the privacy of others.' Wormwood (*A. absinthium*) was one of the chief offenders, its seedlings appearing all over the garden. The herbaceous *A. ludoviciana*, weaving through other plants and growing up to 4 feet was one of the best artemisias for contrast. The smaller *A. stelleriana* (dusty miller) was welcome in high summer, with its dazzling white leaves, as a link between flowers of different colour and type. It was cut back in the autumn so that the following year it made an excellent front-of-border subject, sprawling near the ground with a pretty, softening effect. The now well-known silver beauty, *A. absinthium* 'Lambrook Silver', was the product of a chance mating. It looked spectacular against the dark green of the 'pudding' trees or massed with *A. ludoviciana*. The filigree leaves of *A. canescens* (of gardens) make dense 18-inch high mounds and were extremely effective as an underplanting to old roses. She used *A. pedemontana* in exactly the same way: 'very easy and very lovely ... it walks in a very lady-like way.'

It is unfortunate that many of the best silver plants were not hardy at East Lambrook. *Senecio vira-vira* is one that was given a sheltered home and it usually survived the winter. Another semi-hardy silver is *S. bicolor cineraria* 'White Diamond' which Mrs Fish grew until a better form, *S. b. c.* 'Ramparts', appeared. The latter has the most beautifully cut white chrysanthemum leaves and a graceful form. At East Lambrook it was grown with euphorbias, bergenias and the rose 'Little White Pet'. *Brachyglottis greyi* (formerly *Senecio greyi*) is a hardy silver shrub that Mrs Fish grew in one of the terrace beds. She also grew *B. monroi* and *B. laxifolia* in these beds, finding that they made good clumps to contrast with 'flat' plants.

Achillea clypeolata (of gardens) was called, 'a first-rate silver plant'; 18-inches high with very white ferny foliage and typical yarrow-like flat flower heads in deep yellow from June to August. In contrast, she grew the much smaller *Achillea clavennae*, only 4-inches high, with white flowers and deeply-cut leaves, in paving and walls. Another good silver on walls was *Anaphalis margaritacea* whose silver foliage and pearly-white flowers could spill over the edge in a foaming mass. Another anaphalis, the tall *A. cinnamomea* with willow-like leaves lined with silver, was left uncut in winter because of its handsome frosty appearance. The low-growing *A. triplinervis* with its grey-green foliage, was good all through the year between tall plants, and made an excellent dried flower.

Some grey-leaved plants were especially valued for their powerful architectural qualities. The stately cardoon *Cynara cardunculus* dominated the long border at East Lambrook with its 5-foot stems of silver and branching purple thistle heads. Its cousin *C. scolymus* mixes well and was grown in large clumps in the terrace beds. There are many other characterful silver plants with which she experimented. *Salvia argentea,* also of architectural form, was 'as white as one could wish and with the texture of silk plush.' As it hates rain on its face, she planted it in vertical crevices and removed its flower stems because she thought they were not interesting. The verbascums are on an entirely different scale; in summer their tall flower spikes shoot upwards from the centre of broad mats of felted leaves that can be as large as 2 feet across. Although Mrs Fish liked these plants, she gave up growing *V. bombyciferum* as caterpillars found it irresistible, ruining the appearance of the mats. However, she found that the small-leaved *V. rotundifolium haenseleri* was not so tasty to caterpillars.

Mrs Fish thought that some silver-leaved plants were spoilt by their harsh yellow flowers. She grew 'airy-fairy' *Helichrysum plicatum* by the side of the terrace path, but removed its yellow flowers when they appeared. She treated in the same way *Santolina pinnata neapolitana* that made a graceful feathery white clump against a wall or filled a sheltered corner. *S. p. n.* 'Sulphurea' on the other hand, was allowed to keep its pale yellow flowers. In the case of the curry plant *Helichrysum italicum* (syn *H. angustifolium*) she did not remove its burnished gold flowers because they complemented its fine silver foliage, as did those of the smaller leaved *H. splendidum*. At midsummer the planting at East Lambrook assumed its full richness and complexity but the season was far from over. Late summer was seen by Mrs Fish as an especial challenge and it inspired some of her most imaginative and brilliant schemes.

7

The Mature Garden in Late Summer and Autumn

'One of the first things the gardener has to learn is to look at the garden by the year and not by the week or month ... for me the new season starts in the autumn.'

WHEN MANY PEOPLE are losing enthusiasm for gardening because their gardens are past their best, Mrs Fish was as busy and enthusiastic as ever in hers. Meticulous by nature, she saw the receding summer season and coming autumn as times for reappraising her garden. She tried to observe it objectively: 'I think gardeners should try to keep some time for just looking at their gardens, but I don't suppose they ever will. We have our noses in the earth so much that we don't always see the deficiencies.'

In the late summer the garden at East Lambrook was still full of interest. For many gardeners August is a difficult month – the main summer-flowering season is over and the burnished foliage of autumn is not yet in evidence. At East Lambrook it was the month in which phloxes came into their own. *Phlox paniculata* was very dear to Mrs Fish and she thought it ought to be in every garden. She grew a lavender form of it beside the purple filbert, *Corylus maxima* 'Purpurea' with × *Solidaster* 'Lemore' in front and *Achillea filipendula* 'Gold Plate' behind. The achillea's flat flower heads stood above the phlox and its grey-green foliage softened the whole picture. She also loved the white form, *P. paniculata alba*, preferring it and the species to the many varieties available.

Although their flowers were smaller, she found these two were healthier, lived longer and had 'refinement and charm.' With her characteristically unconventional approach, Mrs Fish thought the way phloxes were grown as border perennials was too stereo-typed. For her they did remarkably well grown in the shade and were most effective among shrubs. For example, the bright salmon-pink *P. paniculata* 'Leo Schlageter' was grown in this way in a shaded border with a violet-purple potentilla. She cut off the flower heads of her phloxes after flowering to encourage their side shoots to flower later in the season.

For more dazzling colour in late summer Mrs Fish grew several kinds of lobelia. As these flower so late in the season, she suggested that they are excellent choices for planting among shrubs, especially against stone walls and among pale-coloured flowers. Many varieties of these tall lobelias were lost during World War II, but subsequently much work was done to reproduce some of the lost colours. She preferred the very old green-leaved *Lobelia cardinalis* rather than the beetroot-coloured types but it did not do as well for her as *L. fulgens*. She grew this in a damp, slightly shaded corner where its brilliant colouring stood out against the dark leaves and white flowers of *Houttuynia cordata* and elsewhere with the fresh green of *Euphorbia pilosa*: 'Get it with the early evening light shining through its plum-coloured leaves and glowing red flowers and you will think your garden is set with jewels.' Mrs Fish thought that lobelias should have plenty of water – preferably rain-water – and that a top-dressing of peat would protect them in all but the most severe winters. *L. syphilitica* in brilliant blue, was very miserable in dry spells but nevertheless survived in a north border. Violet *L.* × *vedrariensis* is tougher and easier than some, holding its starry flowers on stout 18-inch stems. Both these will grow very thickly if the ground is moist enough, producing such impenetrable foliage rosettes that they made good ground cover.

The bergamots, essential plants of the cottage garden, also need moisture but are of a slightly more robust constitution than the lobelias. At East Lambrook they brought welcome splashes of bold colour into the late summer and autumn garden: 'I have always grown as many bergamots as I could, from the tall mauves to the pinks and reds. The tall, leafy stems stand erect and the foliage is aromatic even in mid-winter.' Like the cottagers, she used the leaves to scent her linen and pot-pourri and to flavour tea. Formerly grown in every cottage garden, *Monarda didyma* was 'very voluptuous and satisfying', among other flowers. Newer varieties of bergamot were gaining in popularity but for her the old favourite, *Monarda* 'Cambridge Scarlet' was still the most satisfactory. It could be used not only as a border plant, but as excellent ground cover in a damp site. As a keen collector of white flowers, she considered exceptional the newer variety *M*. 'Snow White', with its green-ruffled white flowers. To show it off she grew it with the greeny-yellow flowers of the golden rod, × *Solidaster* 'Lemore'. Much to her regret, some of the newer named varieties that she grew, proved not to be as resilient as the older ones and, over the years, they were lost.

A group of plants that are very vulnerable in harsh winters, but which Mrs Fish valued nonetheless, are the herbaceous salvias. Even the wild *Salvia pratensis* she thought worthy of inclusion in any garden because of the variety of its flower colour from deep blue through to pink, and for its neat, dark foliage but it did not quite match up to 'the refinement of its coy sister', *Salvia patens*, 'a sow's ear rather than a silk purse.' She grew *S. patens* despite the fact that it has to be lifted every autumn – 'the wonderful blue of its flowers compensate for the trouble.' Her favourite was the majestic *Salvia sclarea turkestanica* with its pale blue flowers surrounded by pink papery bracts. This was one plant that she did not like to see as part of a mass: 'Nothing is more striking than a well-grown plant unencumbered by crowding vegetation.' As this is a biennial, Mrs Fish recommended getting a 'niece' and an 'aunt' to start with, so that one could have flowers continuously. Furthermore, she suggested that some of the unopened flower stems should be cut off to ensure flowers the following year. While she grew this salvia near a group of 'Frensham' roses, it was the long-lasting flowers of *S. haematodes* that made the best companions for the sad pinks and crimsons of old roses: 'No other colour in the garden is quite the same as the silver blue of *S. haematodes*.' Although *S. uliginosa* needs cosseting, Mrs Fish thought that no garden should be without its clear blue flowers. It provides vivid colour in August and September and can 'bring an insipid border to life.' *S. azurea* was valued in the same way: 'When most of the other flowers are calling it a day, these lovely creatures will produce their swaying heads of intense blue above their dying compatriots.' The toughest of the breed was the semi-shrubby *S. grahamii* which she planted near the barton gate in association with a bergenia. At one time, she also grew *S. candelabra* here, where its large woolly leaves and soft lavender-blue flowers were effective with the clusters of small purple flowers of *Verbena rigida*. In a mild year these plants would go on flowering until November.

'Sedums and September go together' – these sturdy plants, such a distinctive feature of gardens in late summer, are valued today as much for the varying colours of their foliage as for their distinctive flat flower heads. Mrs Fish certainly liked their fleshy foliage and recommended them as much for this as for the flowers: 'the use of different coloured foliage takes a garden out of a rut.' At East Lambrook, the small *Sedum* 'Ruby Glow' was one of the first to flower. Mrs Fish liked it for its purple-grey foliage and its ability to make good ground cover at the front of a border. At one time, a fine chance association occurred when seedlings of *Atriplex hortensis rubra* made an appearance behind it. On a larger scale, the plum-coloured foliage of *S. telephium maximum* 'Atro-purpureum' made a perfect background for more brightly-coloured plants. Praising *S.* 'Autumn Joy', Mrs Fish called it one of the most valuable plants ever produced: 'When those large sturdy specimens produce their massive heads of dusky rose red the garden comes alive and the August/September display lasts for several months.' She grew it on one side of *Perovskia atriplicifolia* with *S. telephium* 'Munstead Dark Red' on the other. She liked the various forms of *S. telephium* and suggested that the variegated form could be planted among the aristocrats of the border with a warning that any stems reverting to green must be removed.

'I can hear a gasp of horror when I mention polygonums, but there are several that are well worth growing and do not run too badly.' *P. affine* was one of the most affable of these borderline rampers. It makes good mats of leathery leaves in sun or shade, producing its pink bottle-brush flowers from late summer until autumn frosts, when its rich brown winter leaves take over and help furnish the garden. Although Mrs Fish regarded it as 'capable of high positions in the planting world,' and put it at the front of borders, she also grew it in the inhospitable terrain below the water butts and in the stones beside the drive. She also grew *P. a.* 'Darjeeling Red' but was unconvinced that its brighter flowers were more worthwhile. The tiny *P. vaccinifolium* with small, glossy leaves and soft pink flowers needs to be grown in a broad band to be effective. She grew it in such unprepossessing places as among the stones at the edge of paths. One early-flowering polygonum that was allowed to grow in a shady border was *P. bistorta* 'Superbum'. She grew the type. *P. bistorta* because she enjoyed its bright candy pink and found room for *Reynoutria japonica* and *R. j.* 'Variegata' in the orchard. These, in her day, were classified as polygonums. She was well aware of their bad reputation as runners but found that the former was easily controlled by a sharp spade while the lobster-like 'claws' of the latter's foliage intrigued her.

Like the polygonums, some of the Japanese anemones can be troublesome when their roots burrow into neighbour's territory. Mrs Fish was always mystified that the cottagers managed to grow so many invasive plants and not be overrun with them when she had to work hard to keep all hers in check. She would have loved to grow anemones in the way she had seen in large gardens, where there was enough room to spread into glorious massed effects. In her own garden, she had to settle for small clumps, often placing them beside walls to restrict their root run. The old anemone *A.* × *hybrida* 'Honorine Jobert' (syn. *A.* × *h.* 'Alba') was her first love among the family. She admired the purity of its glistening white single flowers, growing it in association with the rich pink flowers of *Clematis* 'Countess of Onslow'. Mrs Fish liked the pairing of clematis with anemones. The white *A.* × *hybrida* 'Luise Uhink' was grown against a dark curtain of primrose-yellow *Clematis rehderiana* and the soft pink *A. hupehensis* grew in the company of the semi-herbaceous *Clematis heracleifolia* and *Lysimachia clethroides*. This clematis grew over a low wall below the anemone and the group made a lovely picture, both in flower and when the foliage of the clematis and the lysimachia took on gold and russet tints. Although for herself she preferred the simple white anemone, Mrs Fish's visitors were apparently impressed by a deep crimson semi-double she called *A.* × *hybrida* 'Stuttgardia'. She planted this in clumps in the ditch garden with a blue and white monkshood and straw-yellow *A. vulparia*. There were other pink and ruby-coloured Japanese anemones that Mrs Fish liked, one of her favourites being *A. hupehensis* 'Splendens' which has a neater habit than some and associates well with *Viola cornuta*.

While visitors to East Lambrook were impressed with Mrs Fish's anemones, few would have taken much notice of the less glamorous loosestrifes: 'The lysimachias are not a very showy or conspicuous family. People do not say, "You must come and see my lysimachias," as they do their delphiniums, lupins or roses, but these Cinderellas of the flower garden are pleasant and useful.' They begin their long flowering season at the height of summer, becoming more effective as summer recedes and there is less strong colour to mask their subtle charm. Mrs Fish preferred the nobler members of the family but did not dismiss the lowly cottage garden *L. nummularia*: 'If the humble "Creeping Jenny" were a difficult, rare plant we should all rave about it.' She found a place for it and its more refined golden sister, in the ditch garden. The taller native *L. vulgaris*, too invasive and uninteresting for the average border, she thought worth growing in the wilder parts of the garden for its golden autumn foliage. *L. punctata* with its larger flowers and the later-flowering *L. ciliata*, were also useful for filling awkward shady corners. Mrs Fish felt compelled to try *L. leschenaultii* 'for the challenge is irresistible.' Unlike the other loosestrifes, it has rosy-red flowers and is rather tender. The more aristocratic *L. clethroides* with its 'shepherd's crook' white flower spikes, was planted against a wall so that all the 'crooks' had to bend in the same direction. The most aristocratic of the family is undoubtedly the summer-flowering *L. ephemerum*, with glaucous foliage and long-lasting spires of pale grey flowers, described by Mrs Fish as 'a kind grey lady showing up the brilliant colours of other people.'

Most people think of kniphofias as 'Red Hot Pokers' – flaming spikes that overpower many a front garden in late summer. Mrs Fish thought of them in that way until she met the elegant ivory *Kniphofia* 'Maid of Orleans', the green-tipped yellow spires of *K.* 'Wrexham Buttercup' and the pale yellow *K.* 'Brimstone'. These 'dwarf' hybrids start flowering as early as June and may go on well into the autumn. By placing them carefully, Mrs Fish found that their dramatic shapes added an exotic touch to the garden. Of *K. northiae* she wrote, 'when I was given it I did not realise that I was introducing such a surprising plant into the garden.' It makes a great rosette of broad grey-green leaves and the dense flower spikes start as coral buds and open to pineapple heads of greeny-yellow. Mrs Fish put it in her 'green' garden with rue, silver *Cynara cardunculus*, the grass *Carex pendula* and green-burred eryngiums. *K. caulescens* is a smaller, greyer version, flowering in early autumn on elephant trunk stems that loll on the ground. Mrs Fish suggested that both these should be grown as specimens, as in a border 'they and the other plants would feel a little embarrased.'

Little orange *K. triangularis* (syn. *K. galpinii*) and *K. thompsonii snowdenii* are autumn flowering. The latter sends up bright coral torches to the end of October and, being the only runner in the family, is easily propagated. When she first planted *K.* 'Prince Igor' in a border filled with perfectly civilised and well-proportioned plants, she did not know what she was letting herself in for. Its towering 5-feet spikes of glowing orange dwarfed everything around it, but total embarrassment was spared by the delicate contrast of a neighbouring variegated kerria (*K. japonica* 'Picta'). Later, she removed the Prince and gave him a solitary seat under a pollarded catalpa. Having learned a lesson about the placing of kniphofias, Mrs Fish planted the coral and lemon *K. rooperi* in the suitable company of *Acer platanoides* 'Goldsworth Purple'. The larger kniphofias looked best growing alone in rough grass where their ungainly foliage was not so obtrusive as in the border. Scarlet *K.* 'Samuel's Sensation', *K. rooperi* and *K.* 'Prince Igor' were suitable candidates for this treatment. The more elegant types such as deep primrose *K.* 'Gold Else', pale orange *K. galpinii*, *K.* 'Maid of Orleans' and *K.* 'Modesta' all blended harmoniously with other plants if placed at the back of borders where she could 'let them rise out of a sea of green.'

As the summer days faded into autumn, Mrs Fish positively relished the work that this time of year brought: 'For me the new season starts in the autumn: I always regard the precious months before Christmas as the beginning and not the end of the year.' This was the time when she rearranged borders to improve colour schemes, moved precious items if they seemed unhappy, thinned out over-zealous members of the community, thickened up stragglers and planted any new arrivals. It was the time for her to take stock; planning and planting went hand in hand because she thought it better to plant in the autumn; plants had a chance to settle down before the ground lost its heat and if there was not time to finish everything, then there would always be time in the spring.

'To me chrysanthemums belong to the autumn, their scent goes with the smell of bonfires and wet leaves.' Chrysanthemums are another example of the kind of plant whose old varieties Mrs Fish really appreciated, while still seeking out what she considered to be the best of the newer ones. Unfortunately, she found the tall cottage chrysanthemums straggly in growth and impossible to grow straight, even when staked. The best way to grow them, she discovered, was through the supporting stems of a sturdy shrub or tied back to a wall. *C.* 'Emperor of China' was given this treatment and in this way its shaded pink flowers on crimson-tinted foliage did not get knocked down or ruined by autumn winds. An old yellow chrysanthemum was grown through *Anaphalis cinnamomea* so its soft yellow flowers mingled with the fluffy white heads and silver foliage of the anaphalis. A shorter single pink she found easier to accommodate among border plants was *C.* 'Innocence' which she rescued from an old garden and named. Her favourite was the late-flowering, scented *C.* 'Wedding Day'. Its single white daisies with green, instead of the usual yellow, centres, were given the soft grey-green *Phlomis fruticosa* for support.

Grown not for its flowers, but for the effect of its brilliant golden foliage, *Tanacetum parthenium aureum* (formerly *Chrysanthemum parthenium*) is a free-seeding plant. As she liked to put silver and gold together, Mrs Fish collected the seedlings and grouped them as a foil for silver plants such as *Helichrysum stoechas barrelieri* and *Artemisia absinthium* 'Lambrook Silver'. The tough and resilient *Tanacetum macrophyllum* (formerly *Chrysanthemum macrophyllum*) was grown for another purpose; its monochrome colouring meant that it mixed easily with other plants, with its off-white flowers on 4-foot stems of feathery leaves, it made a perfect back-of-border plant. Another example of the revaluation of an old and worthy plant is the giant *Leucanthemella serotina* (formerly *Chrysanthemum uliginosum*). This, with large single white flowers with greenish-yellow centres, was one of the first plants given to Mrs Fish by a local villager. It made an impressive autumn picture with lavender-blue *Aster × frikartii* and *Kniphofia rooperi*, whose broad flower spikes start orange-red and open to greeny-yellow.

Michaelmas daisies were the cottager's choice to flower with chrysanthemums. Mrs Fish was selective with asters, knowing that many were too pushy for her crowded borders. She preferred the old *Aster novi-belgii* 'Climax' to any of the newer ones: 'In a class by itself.' It is vigorous and elegant, bearing pyramids of spode-blue single flowers over a long period. As its name signifies, *A. tradescantii* is a veteran plant and one much admired by Mrs Fish: 'I wonder what I did before I had it.' She had found it in a little garden not far from East Lambrook, and in its new home gave it a sheltered corner where it opened its miniature white daisies late in the season. *A. macrophyllus* has the palest lilac flowers and spreading roots, and it was used as ground cover under the small pink Floribunda rose 'Radium'. *A. tongolensis* 'Napsbury' gave striking violet, orange-centred daisies in summer and formed thick mats of dark, shining leaves in autumn. Referring to the way in which the smaller Michaelmas daisies were traditionally grown, Mrs Fish wrote: 'How often we admire the wide borders of mauve or pink in autumn. They grow evenly and thickly, and, if instead of straight borders, they are planted to fill in the space between trees and shrubs (wide plantings that taper off into the background), no cover could be more effective or more cheerful.'

Some of her asters were slow to increase. Among them, *A. lateriflorus* 'Horizontalis' she thought worthy of cosseting. Its small lavender flowers with crimson centres, flower all the way up its 2-foot stems and its very small leaves turn coppery-purple in early autumn. For a long display she liked *A.* × *frikartii* 'Wunder von Stäfa', placing it with the pale pink *Penstemon* 'Pennington Gem' or coral *P. isophyllus*. Of the smaller asters, *A. sedifolius nanus*, forming a neat dome of starry blue in late summer, was treasured by Mrs Fish, who thought it suitable for the rock garden or at the front of a bed with pink or red penstemons.

'I do not think there is any excuse for the October garden to be dull. Cimicifugas flower extremely late but it is worth waiting for them.' They are striking plants, with bottle-brush flowers and ferny foliage, which can reach 5 feet in height. They are suitable for growing in herbaceous borders or with trees and shrubs, but must have damp growing conditions. Mrs Fish grew *C. racemosa cordifolia*, which was by no means the most impressive of the family, having rather dull creamy flowers and the smaller, but more elegant *C. simplex* 'White Pearl' that starts flowering in September but continues right through autumn. *C. racemosa*, a species from North America, is the earliest of the family to flower, with its graceful white 'brushes' rising above beautifully cut foliage. Mrs Fish enjoyed this and the even more spectacular *C. ramosa*, that can grow to 6 feet with tapering white feathery flowers in September and October.

An old cottage plant of which Mrs Fish was very fond was the 'obedient plant', *Physostegia virginiana*: 'it is strange that there are still gardens where physostegia isn't grown.' The plant's name comes from the way its hinged flower stalks will stay put when moved. Mrs Fish liked best *P. v.* 'Vivid', that flowers from late summer well into autumn and has deep pink tubular flowers similar to a snapdragon. She grew the tall *P. v.* 'Summer Spire' in deep lilac-purple, with *Brachyglottis monroi* (syn. *Senecio monroi*), a dark green senecio with silvery undersides to its leaves. Two other out-of-the-ordinary but subdued plants that flower in October, Mrs Fish described as having 'character and charm' – *Calamintha nepeta nepeta* (syn. *C. nepetoides*) and *Scutellaria indica parvifolia*, both of which she first saw growing at Hidcote. The calamintha is a neat little foot-high bush, covered with soft, pale lavender flowers and Mrs Fish thought it a fairly easy plant to please. The scutellaria she planted in a damp site where its spreading grey foliage and deep lilac flowers added charm in their small way.

While the spring was obviously the time when bulbs played their greatest role in the garden, there were many autumn-flowering bulbous plants that Mrs Fish used to give colour late in the year. She particularly liked the exotic-looking South African Kaffir lilies and wrote about their delights more than once: 'It always surprises me that more people do not grow these delightful crimson flags.' Although they are hardier than they appear, they demand moist conditions and Mrs Fish was careful to stress this to her readers. Her favourite was *Shizostylis coccinea* 'Mrs Hegarty', with gladiolus-like deep pink flowers and pale strap leaves. The later flowering and more robust *S.c.* 'Viscountess Byng', with satin pink flowers, was also an inhabitant of the garden and Mrs Fish recalled that she had 'picked a bunch of these delicate pink flowers on Christmas Day in a year when we had no bad frosts until the New Year.' Also from South Africa, the crocosmias provided stronger colour but similar form at this time of year. At East Lambrook there was both the small, hardy red-flowered *C. pottsii* and the much larger *C. paniculata* (syn. *Curtonus paniculatus*) with small orange flowers, with *Euphorbia dulcis* making a vividly tinted companion. The lily-like *Nerine bowdenii*, yet another South African native, also provided bright flowers for the autumn: 'There is something rather exotic and hot-housy about them that makes the proud owner wonder, "Did I really grow that lovely thing?"' She grew hers as a fringe in a narrow border below a south-facing wall right by the house.

A group that Mrs Fish grew for its quiet refinement and intriguingly-marked flowers were the toad lilies. They start flowering in September when their unobtrusive flowers get more attention than they would at the height of summer. The first ones Mrs Fish grew were *Tricyrtis hirta* and its white form, *T. h. alba* of which she later confessed, 'I do not think it says much for my intelligence that I chose the white form of a plant that is characterised by the strange spotting of the flowers.' To these she added three other species, *T. macropoda*, *T. latifolia* and *T. formosana* Stolonifera group (syn. *T. stolonifera*). The one Mrs Fish liked best for its distinctive Japanese character was *T. macropoda* with its greenish yellow flowers blotched with purple, and deeply ribbed leaves. She grew it in shade that suited it well, with as companions *Thalictrum delavayi* and *Artemisia absinthium* 'Lambrook Silver'.

Just as the evergreen shrubs had done in the winter and spring garden, the hydrangeas made a strong impression in the autumn: 'All through the late autumn and nearly till Christmas the bread and-butter hydrangeas are extremely beautiful and add much richness to the garden.' She liked the way the leaves turned colour beautifully and the flowers changed into delicious soft shades. When she first planted them in the front garden, she stuck to the hortensia types, in pinks and whites, later adding the odd bush with variegated leaves. It was only when she had become an accomplished gardener that she started adding the more unusual species to the garden. She could never decide whether she preferred the hortensia hydrangeas to the lacecaps. In general, she thought the larger lacecaps like *H. macrophylla* 'Mariesii' better in a woodland setting where they could grow unrestrictedly, preferring to use the more upright forms of *H. serrata* in beds among other plants. Her favourite was *H. s.* 'Grayswood', with bright lace-cap flowers and crimson leaves. The centres of the flowers are blue but the sterile flowers around the edge may be white turning to pink, crimson or blue. At East Lambrook, it was grown with *Clematis × jouiniana* 'Praecox' and a mallow, *Malva alcea fastigiata*. Not having extensive woodland she grew *H. macrophylla* 'Mariesii' in a north east corner of the front garden where it thrived: 'a most sumptuous spectacle with glorious foliage spreading far and wide and tier upon tier of great colourful flowers.' *H. aspera villosa* was also grown in the front garden where its pale purple flowers were especialy welcome. She was less enthusiastic about the climbing *H. petiolaris*: 'lovely when in full bloom but looks miserable when it has finished flowering', but grew it nonetheless to disguise an unnattractive stucco extension. Here it was paired with a wall shrub, *Cotoneaster lacteus*, with grey-green foliage and crimson berries that made a fine vertical carpet for the white flowers and bare stems of the hydrangea. Mrs Fish had no reservations about *H. involucrata* 'Hortensis' with its double pink flowers: 'because of its loveliness, it gets a prominent position in the garden.' Because they gave winter interest the flower heads of hydrangeas were left on the plants until spring, only those that she needed for dried flower arrangements in the house were removed.

'It is not only the flowers that bring colour to the October garden. Berries and leaves make vivid patches of colour, colour that in the case of some of the berries lasts well into winter.' A favourite shrub for autumn and winter was *Photinia davidiana undulata* (syn. *Stranvaesia d. u.*). Although it has clusters of pretty white flowers in the summer, it was for its glorious leaf colour and brilliant crimson berries that she wanted it. Many of the shrubs and small trees she grew were commonplace, but were just as effective as the few maples she had. Several of the snowberry clan were planted under apple trees in the orchard where they covered themselves in luminous white or pink fruits in the autumn. The deciduous spindleberries also contributed to the late season with their bright berries and good autumn colour while the pinnate foliage of the stag's horn sumach, *Rhus typhina*, turned shades of orange-red. Certainly there was much to see and admire at this time of year, but Mrs Fish was also moved by the scents of autumn: 'Bonfires and wet leaves, the aromatic fragrances of wild strawberries and the strong scent of violet-leaved *Hebe cupressoides* fills the air with incense and this is always stronger in autumn and winter.'

Mrs Fish rarely had time to enjoy the sights and smells of her garden as a spectator rather than as a worker. She was far too disciplined to let herself waste a moment and the autumn was that time in the year when the garden demanded most of her physically: 'Because the work is heavy, the short days are a blessing, and how welcome the fire when we leave the garden in the dusk.'

8

The Garden Today

IN THE LAST three chapters we have described Margery Fish's garden as it was in its heyday. Many of the plants that she used in her characteristic way are still there to be seen. Any garden may lose its character when its maker dies – particularly one as fragile and personal as that at East Lambrook Manor. But, miraculously, its precious atmosphere of intimacy and privacy has been preserved. For today's gardeners, this is fortunate because the importance of Mrs Fish is hard to overestimate. Her philosophy is as relevant now as it was when she was gardening. Her emphasis on all-the-year gardening with ease of maintenance in mind, while stressing the importance of preserving and sharing herbaceous plants, is timeless and can be copied by anyone, whether they have a large or small garden. That the garden has not only survived but flourishes and is developing under its present ownership is a tale worth telling.

After Mrs Fish's death in 1969 the estate passed to her nephew, Henry Boyd-Carpenter, who realised that he had inherited a garden of unique complexity needing the unremitting care of a dedicated and knowledgeable gardener. When he took over there were well over two thousand different plants in the garden, many of which were not labelled or whose positions only Mrs Fish had known. Often there was more than one form of the same plant, some of which were known simply as 'Mrs So-and-So's' after the person who had given it to her. There were, for example, seven different forms of *Pulmonaria rubra*. Furthermore there were large collections of hellebores and snowdrops, many of which could not be identified easily, even by experts. Many of the double primroses were hidden under larger plants in the ditch garden and there was no map showing where or what they all were. Confronted with complexities such as these, Mr Boyd-Carpenter consulted expert gardeners about whether it would be possible, or even desirable, to save the garden. It was generally felt that it was absolutely essential that such a unique collection of herbaceous plants should be preserved and some of those consulted, like Christopher Brickell, Fred Whitsey and Valerie Finnis, later gave very valuable help with the naming of plants.

Out of loyalty to Mrs Fish, her gardeners stayed on and were immensely helpful during this difficult period. Maureen Whitty, who had worked for Mrs Fish since 1964, was able to help locate plants and, as an expert propagator, to keep the nursery going. Jean Goscomb, Mrs Fish's secretary/gardener from 1965, and Jean Burgess, who had come as a secretary in 1958 and then went on to work in the nursery, also provided invaluable information and help. However, although they had all worked for Mrs Fish for some time, their duties had been principally in the nursery and not in the garden itself. Mrs Fish had always been willing to show them plants and instruct them about the garden, but she was reluctant to let them weed or plant in it. Therefore, they did not get to know the garden with anything like the intimacy that she did and found it very difficult to work there without her guidance and influence. However, for the next sixteen years the garden was kept up, and opened regularly to the public. From 1971 Henry Boyd-Carpenter's parents went to live in the house and assumed responsibility for the garden and the running of the nursery, and although they were very keen to do the job, it was really too much for people of their age. Mrs Fish may have written about carefree gardening and the labour-saving merits of ground cover plants, but as they discovered, her own garden was a complicated and finely balanced organism that was anything but labour-saving. To keep it in balance, restraining the rampant while mothering the temperamental, required the constant attention of someone who knew it intimately. Indeed, even Mrs Fish had not been able to keep pace with it once her other activities took up so much of her time and her health started to fail. Certainly Mr and Mrs Boyd-Carpenter were very able gardeners but they did not have Mrs Fish's exceptional capabilities or knowledge and, when they took on the garden, did not fully understand how to continue her style of gardening. Sadly, despite all their efforts, the garden gradually began to lose some of its atmosphere as many of its rarities were lost or swamped. Had it not been for them, however, there is little doubt that the garden would have been irretrievably lost. By 1984, when they had both died, the problem of maintaining the garden became acute. Although it was a painful prospect, Henry Boyd-Carpenter decided to sell the house and its garden because he felt that it was impossible to combine his career in London with all the work needed to run the estate properly. The impending sale prompted the gardening press to write about the garden and there was much interest all over the country in finding ways of saving it – such was the lasting affection for Mrs Fish and her creation. Further publicity was given to the garden by the fact that English Heritage had just completed its listing of English gardens and East Lambrook was listed Grade I, making it one of only 100 gardens in the country to merit the top category.

The estate was sold in 1984 and by the greatest good fortune its new owners, Andrew and Dodo Norton, are knowledgeable and dedicated gardeners, who are determined to re-establish the distinctive character of the garden. Andrew Norton's mother was a devoted follower of Mrs Fish and bought many plants from her nursery. The Nortons moved in during August 1985 and had few illusions about the size of their task. They already had some experience of garden restoration but nothing remotely as complicated as East Lambrook. When they arrived, although the bones of the garden were more or less intact, its focus had become blurred and countless distinctive plants had been lost.

Their instinct was to leave the garden untouched for a year, during which they could observe it closely, to see what each season brought. Their earlier experience had taught them the dangers of rushing in and making possibly irrevocable changes too quickly. They realised too that the restoration would be expensive and they needed time to see how best to run the nursery to put it on a sound financial footing. Furthermore, to help cover the costs of running the garden, they had to find ways of attracting more than the 2000 visitors who came in their first year, without changing the intimate character of the garden which is vital to it.

In the nursery the Nortons planned to make Mrs Fish's original plant-list the basis of a new one. However, they found that many of the plants she made popular and sold in the nursery are now in general cultivation; a tribute to her powers of advocacy. Therefore, to form the core of the new list and to give the nursery a distinct identity, they decided to select a group of plants that are still associated with Mrs Fish's name, but which appeal to today's gardeners. The cranesbills appeared to be the perfect choice, as they are an extensive and versatile group and offer possiblities for future hybridisation. They have been particular favourites of Mr Norton's since as a boy he first noticed them in the wild. He still thinks that 'the meadow cranesbill is one of the loveliest plants there is.' Four years on, there are now over 60 different geraniums for sale and the garden has become the keeper of one of the National Collections. For a small, specialist nursery there were the unexpected problems of national publicity. There was so much interest generated by an article Fred Whitsey wrote for *The Daily Telegraph* about the nursery's proposed specialisation in geraniums that the Nortons received 2,000 enquiries. Not yet having enough stock ready for dispatch, they had to write to everyone with a list of geraniums which would be available in time. Besides the geraniums, the other early stalwarts of the nursery were primroses and hellebores. However, these were more difficult, as the primroses were hard to find and the hellebores in the garden had hybridised so much. Today, the Nortons' improved propagation techniques are so successful that the nursery's list contains over 500 plants, with emphasis on cottage garden plants of the sort Mrs Fish used, silver- and grey-leaved plants, euphorbias and salvias, as well as geraniums.

On taking over the garden, Mr and Mrs Norton found that its greatest asset was its loyal and dedicated gardening staff. At that time there was the head gardener, Mark Staimer – who had joined the staff during the Boyd-Carpenter's time – an assistant gardener and five part-time women helpers, one of whom was Mrs Burgess. As she had worked for Mrs Fish since 1958 and had stayed on with the Boyd-Carpenters, she provided a link between the past and present garden, giving the kind of continuity that is so valuable when restoring a garden of this sort. Within a short time of their arrival, she introduced the Nortons to two of Mrs Fish's former gardeners, Maureen Whitty and Jean Goscomb, who were also keen to help in any way they could. Miss Whitty agreed to rejoin the staff part time and, thanks to the very valuable notes she made about the plants in the garden soon after Mrs Fish's death, together with her remarkable memory for the siting and relationship of plants, she has played a key role in the garden's restoration.

Before work could begin, the Nortons realised that they needed to do a great deal of research on what had been grown and how the garden had developed in Mrs Fish's time. Naturally they read all her books and had transcripts of many of her articles. In addition they have built up a collection of slides that Mrs Fish had used for lecturing and reference. They retrieved 1,200 from various sources with the help of Mr Boyd-Carpenter, friends and the National Council for the Conservation of Plants and Gardens (NCCPG) which takes a helpful interest in the problems of restoring gardens. By studying the books, articles and slides and consulting Mrs Fish's gardeners, they started to put on computer a list of plants she grew. The slides also proved invaluable in the lengthy process of identification of those items still in the garden. It soon became obvious just how many plants had gone missing since Mrs Fish's death and, to regain the garden's character, it was essential to retrieve as many as possible. This process was started with Maureen Whitty's help; she was still in touch with some of the other plantsmen and women who grew Mrs Fish's plants and who she knew would share what they had.

Once the restoration was under way, Mr Norton decided that publicity would be helpful. He encouraged the gardening press to write about the work and spread the word himself by writing and talking to as many contacts as possible. An article he wrote for the NCCPG magazine, including a list of missing plants, aroused enormous interest. The response to this request and all the publicity was immediate and generous. Letters of encouragement, offers of help and, most importantly, plants, arrived from all over the United Kingdom and even from abroad. Four years later, plants are still arriving at East Lambrook – as many as 1,000 in a year. Mr Norton says that, at first, he made the mistake of planting arrivals straight into the garden itself; sadly he lost track of where he had put many of them because other plants kept appearing where he least expected them. Now, all new plants are grown on in a holding bed until they are well-established. Having propagated enough for the garden or the nursery, they can then be given a permanent home within the garden where they are carefully and unobtrusively labelled with a number that can be checked against a master list.

It had been Mr Norton's plan to organise the running of the garden so that he could take time off if he needed to and the garden's survival would become less dependent on the skills of one person. However, he soon discovered, like the Boyd-Carpenters before him, that the garden demands a very personal, day-to-day involvement. If he leaves it for more than a few days, the detrimental effect is noticeable: 'There is so much intimate gardening to be done – the concept of an all-the-year garden makes enormous demands'. As the garden is open all the year round and each area is planted to provide interest in all the seasons, tidiness, on which Mrs Fish herself had been so insistent, is of paramount importance. There are so many plants grown within a small space, it is a perennial problem to keep everything in balance. Mrs Fish's idea of a carefree garden, with good ground cover to suppress weeds and retain moisture, works, but removing dead foliage, dead heading and cutting back the overgrowth are unrelenting jobs. Certainly, many of the plants look after themselves but others that are too invasive must be controlled to prevent their swamping less vigorous plants. Seed collection is another time-consuming occupation that is very important for the future of the garden. Mr Norton confesses that the garden is 'the most labour-intensive one you could possibly create.' Fortunately he has an efficient and dedicated team of gardeners and helpers – today there are two full-time gardeners and eight part-timers, and he and his wife spend an immense amount of time in the garden. Furthermore, the Nortons believe that there should always be someone available to talk to visitors, many of whom have travelled long distances.

The Nortons have made subtle alterations to the surroundings of the garden. They thought it important that nursery and garden should not be divorced from each other, so they made a new public entrance through the nursery and laid a curving path from it, through the orchard and into the garden. The previous entrance had been through the barton gate which made a rather abrupt and inconvenient approach. To improve the orchard's look, a beech hedge was planted on one side of the path and climbing and rambler roses – *R.* 'Rambling Rector', *R. filipes*

'Kiftsgate' and *R. brunonii* planted beneath the fruit trees on the other. To give the visitors something to admire when the roses were not flowering, the trees were underplanted with small narcissi, fritillaries, cowslips and autumn-flowering cyclamen.

As spring arrived after the Nortons' first winter at East Lambrook, the reality of what they had undertaken became apparent. Hundreds of astrantia and geranium seedlings, thickets of new bergenia leaves, brambles and weeds burst into life about them. In this eruption of foliage, they were delighted to discover hidden treasures emerging – an enormous range of bulbs, particularly snowdrops, hellebores of every colour and type, including a rare double purple, a variegated *Geranium reflexum* and many other welcome reminders of the great gardener whose world they now inhabited. By the end of the summer, Mr Norton felt that he had begun to appreciate more clearly what Mrs Fish's overall concept had been and how each area, distinct as it was, should be linked to the next. The definition she intended had been lost over the years and he saw the task as one of reclaiming the unique identity of the garden, area by area, following Mrs Fish's planting as closely as possible. As restoration involves so much work, he thought it best to tackle only one or two areas at a time. Because the garden had become so muddled, the plants in each area being restored were moved to holding beds, where they could be sifted and identified, to avoid the loss of anything precious. The plan was to propagate any plant of merit they discovered and when good stocks were produced, to re-establish it in the garden.

One of the first areas to be tackled was the long border beneath the eastern boundary wall. It appeared to be beyond saving as it was choked with bindweed and ground elder. It was cleared completely, any plants worth keeping preserved, and left fallow for a year. In Mrs Fish's time, the trees at the back of the border were immature and the border was therefore relatively sunny. Today, there is a certain amount of shade and the tree roots have invaded the top soil, limiting the number of shrubs that can be grown. No garden stands still and this change in the environment of a particular part of the garden is typical of the problems which any garden restorer faces. Maureen Whitty, who was given the job of replanting this border, has succeeded in recreating the essence of Mrs Fish's scheme. Her idea was to let the plants intermingle to achieve a soft, informal effect using foliage contrasts and silver-leaved plants among soft coloured flowers – pinks, blues and yellows – with the occasional brighter or darker colour to lift the planting. The first of the 300 plants that were chosen was the giant silver cardoon, *Cynara cardunculus*, that dominated the border in Mrs Fish's day. Planted in assocation are blue and white *Campanula lactiflora*, purple and white *Penstemon* 'Alice Hindley', the small white daisies of *Tanacetum parthenium* 'White Bonnet', *Penstemon* 'Andenken an Friedrich Hahn' (syn. *P.* 'Garnet') and *Eryngium alpinum*, used here for its striking steel blue flower heads. In front of the cardoon, *Sedum telephium maximum* and *S. t. m.* 'Atropurpureum' make a strong contrast with their fleshy leaves and flat pinky-purple flower heads. Mrs Fish enjoyed putting purple foliage and pink flowers together in her schemes and today there is a bush of purple sage behind the trailing *Polygonum capitatum* with its marbled bronze leaves and pink flowers that appear from early summer. As a concession to Walter Fish's taste, three roses ('Aloha', 'Paul's Scarlet Climber' and 'Pauls's Perpetual White') have been trained up poles placed at intervals along the border, giving height and contrast to the mixed planting beneath. Among the special plants here is the rare double *Delphinium* 'Alice Artindale', grown in partnership with a rose-pink hollyhock and the bright blue flowers of *Linum narbonense*. Nearby, *Artemisia arborescens* 'Faith Raven' acts as a delicate foil for the blue campanula, *C. lactiflora* 'Pouffe', the pink *Geranium endressii*, *Iris pallida* 'Variegata' and *Eryngium bourgatii* with its blue flower-heads surrounded by long silvery bracts. Following Mrs Fish's principle of structure in borders provided by interesting foliage, Maureen Whitty has contrasted *Paeonia delavayi lutea* with *Phlomis fruticosa*, a golden privet and groups of *Euphorbia characias wulfenii*. Rising over this group are the purple leaves of the sycamore, *Acer platanoides* 'Goldsworth Purple' enlivened by the pink-flowered *Clematis montana* 'Elizabeth'. On the wall behind, the rambling rose 'Goldfinch' in white and yellow, completes the picture. As Mrs Fish would have liked, the wall behind the border is well covered, but not hidden, with climbers – the soft yellow of the rose 'Mermaid', and creamy-white *Clematis* 'Miss Bateman'; the startling red of the rose 'American Pillar' is matched in richness by the dark purple of *Clematis* × *jackmanii* and softened by the blue clematis, *C.* × *jouiniana* 'Mrs. Robert Brydon';

further along the wall, *Clematis* 'Perle d'Azur' grows through the semi-evergreen *Lonicera japonica* 'Halliana'. For interest in the early spring, there are crocuses, scillas and tulips – as well as ground cover in the form of pulmonarias, tellimas and the early flowers of doronicums, *Omphalodes cappadocica*, hellebores and primroses.

Work started on the ditch and silver garden at the same time. The silver garden is now bigger than in Mrs Fish's day, having been extended to take in the cottage annexe's little garden. It is also more emphatically silver, with room to grow larger groups of Mrs Fish's best silver-leaved plants. To the familiar artemisias which we have mentioned before have been added rarer ones – the creeping *A. gracilis*, grey-felted *A. tridentata* and *A. ludoviciana incompta* (syn. *A. discolor*) with its thread-like foliage. Helichrysums do well here, with the shrubby *Helichrysum stoechas*, *H. ambiguum*, *H. fontanesii* and *H. sibthorpii*. Plants with soft, furry silver leaves contrast well with the filigree foliage of artemisias and helichrysums and are well represented. The most dramatic of these is *Salvia argentea*, a plant much admired by Mrs Fish. Of course, there is that other silver stalwart of hers – *Stachys byzantina* 'Silver Carpet', and the noble verbascums that caused her so much anxiety when caterpillars feasted on their leaves. The woolly-leaved *Ballota pseudodictamnus* – recommended for planting to fall over a low wall – here softens the paving. Scent delighted Mrs Fish and the silver garden today is full of intensely aromatic plants – the various artemisias, lavenders, old pinks, and the curry plant, *Helichrysum italicum*. To give structure, the silver foliage shrubs *Phlomis lanata*, *Brachyglottis greyi* and *Olearia moschata* have all been included and, as soft contrasts, there are the pink flowers of roses, *Helianthemum* 'Wisley Pink' and a bindweed, *Convolvulus althaeoides*. Following Mrs Fish, the Nortons remove from their silver-foliage plants any flowers that are too stridently yellow.

Identification of the ditch's snowdrop collection has proved difficult; there are so many clumps appearing each season, even the experts have had difficulty sorting out the hybrids from the species and original garden varieties. Now as each clump is identified, it is labelled and logged. The primroses, like the snow-drops, were one of the features of the ditch in Mrs Fish's time, but have proved to be some of the most difficult plants to replace. However, thanks to the generosity of specialist growers and

amateur enthusiasts, they are gradually coming back to the
garden. On a May morning's walk along the bottom of the ditch,
one can now see some that Mrs Fish knew well and other, newer
varieties. There is the bright pink 'Kinlough Beauty', described
lovingly by her as looking as though 'it should be in every cottage
garden'; the old Irish 'Tawny Port', that she found difficult to
keep – a dwarf beauty, with dark wine flowers and maroon-green
foliage; the large crimson and gold 'Salamander', a Jack-in-the-
Green variety, and another – 'Tipperary Purple', both of which
she grew. The 'Garryard' primrose, 'Guinevere', with its pale
lilac flowers with a yellow eye and typical bronze tinted foliage
has been retrieved too. Another of the same type, 'Enchantress'
was found by the Nortons, then lost; the primroses' fickle nature
means that they disappear without warning. But the Nortons
have reintroduced many which were feared lost to cultivation.
One of these was the double mauve, white-edged 'Prince Silverwings' that was found in a private garden in Ledbury. Another
was the single 'Miss Massey' – 'a virile person', Mrs Fish called
her, that was re-discovered in the Savill Garden. Pam Gossage,
a specialist in growing primroses, has retrieved many more.

With the hellebores there was quite a different problem. It was
not that they had disappeared, rather that they had hybridised
to such an extent that identification was extremely difficult, often
impossible. Originally, many of them were grown in the shaded
ground between the ditch and the orchard – a site that must have
suited them well, as they had done their best to colonise the whole
area. Again, Mr Norton has called on the help of private collectors
to provide species and named varieties.

Although Mrs Fish had made a white garden but abandoned
it, Mr Norton decided to re-establish it because he shares her
passion for white flowers and thinks they are most effective when
grown in semi-shade with carefully selected greens and green-
and-white variegated foliage. Building on the structure provided
by Mrs Fish's original planting of a *Magnolia stellata*, *M.* × *soulangeana*, *Amelanchier canadensis*, *Cornus mas* 'Variegata' and silver
birches, he has added many plants that seem quite happy to grow
in this shady, sheltered situation. These include *Cistus hirsutus
psilosepalus*, and the geraniums *G. sylvaticum album*, *G. sanguineum
album* and the starry-flowered white form of herb Robert, *G.
robertianum* 'Celtic White'. Among the bulbous plants are *Anemone*

narcissiflora, *Liriope muscari* 'Alba', *Crocus tommasinianus albus* and white colchicums. Ground cover is provided by three forms of the white-flowered pulmonaria, white brunnera, white-variegated lamium and a double-flowered variegated form of the wild strawberry. *Clematis* 'Duchess of Edinburgh' grows happily through the *Magnolia* × *soulangeana* while *C.* 'Margot Koster' winds itself round the trunk of *Prunus* × *subhirtella* 'Autumnalis'.

The green garden, too, has been extensively replanted. When Mrs Fish created it, there was not so much shade as there is today, and therefore it is no longer possible to grow some of the sun-loving plants that she did. By the time the Nortons started work, it had disappeared under a sea of astrantias and the evergreen foliage of *Vinca major hirsuta*, but they have now recaptured much of its original flavour. One of Mrs Fish's exotics, the palm *Trachycarpus fortunei*, still dominates the front of the garden and her Glastonbury hawthorn has grown very tall, as has the blue cedar in the background. An attractive alder with finely-cut leaves, *Alnus glutinosa* 'Imperialis' and a white Judas tree, *Cercis siliquastrum* 'Alba', also Fish originals, cast their shade too. Beneath the trees, a green tapestry has been woven using the green alpine strawberry 'Plymouth Strawberry', variegated honesty, pale astrantias – particularly 'Shaggy' – periwinkles and geraniums. Among the plants that have been replaced here are many of Mrs Fish's favourites – *Bupleurum angulosum*, *Veratrum viride*, *Galtonia princeps*, the green-flowered rose, *Rosa* 'Viridiflora' and *Helleborus* 'Greenland'.

There is still much work to be done. The terraces have proved to be the biggest problem because, being visible from all sides, their planting is difficult to arrange. Mr Norton thinks it is very important to reclaim their perspective by judiciously removing some shrubs and trees that block the overall view. Also he has to decide whether to replace Mrs Fish's 'pudding trees' that had been allowed to grow too big in past years. Although he has cut them back without losing their shape, he thinks they may still be out of proportion to their surroundings and so is growing on some replacements. Within the flower beds, he hopes to recreate Mrs Fish's tapestry effect, using herbaceous plants with the occasional tree or shrub. The planting will be more difficult because the terraces are laid out in a north-east, south-west direction and the obliquely falling light adds unexpected shadows and highlights.

Work has recently started on the Lido, which, together with the Coliseum at the bottom of the terraces, Mr Norton sees as an ideal site for special treasures. Planting has begun on the banks of the Lido with unusual plants like *Aster tradescantii*, *Ajuga pyramidalis* 'Metallica Crispa', clumps of double sweet rocket (*Hesperis matronalis alba* double form, a plant very nearly lost to cultivation but recently rediscovered), smaller grasses and rare double primroses. The sundial garden, probably untouched since Mrs Fish's day, presents a serious problem. It has become congested with geranium seedlings, hellebores, irises and perennial sweet peas and as the soil is exceptionally heavy, a considerable amount of conditioning will have to be done. Unlike Mrs Fish, Mr Norton does not put home-made compost on the garden because of the risk of weed seed surviving in it. At present, he uses it only on the nursery stock beds, preferring to put well-rotted manure and bonemeal on the flower beds in autumn and a mulch of old potting medium in spring. The area alongside the ditch garden, known as the Strip, also offers scope for improvement and the plan includes the replanting or replacement of the roses grown there.

The Nortons believe that it would be quite wrong to treat East Lambrook as a horticultural mausoleum. They feel that it should be seen to exemplify the Fish style while evolving as all gardens must. For this reason they are continuing to introduce plants they believe Mrs Fish would have liked. For example in the green garden alone they have added the green lavender, *Lavandula viridis*, a new 'poker' with yellowish-white torches, *Kniphofia* 'Little Maid' and two coronillas – *Coronilla glauca* and *C. glauca* '*Variegata*' for their delicate foliage. Furthermore, just as Mrs Fish felt compelled to encourage people's enthusiasm so Mr and Mrs Norton believe that the garden should continue to inspire gardeners today.

Appendix

Margery Fish's Writing

ONE OF THE reasons that Mrs Fish's ideas caught on so quickly was because her writing had immediate appeal to a broad cross-section of the gardening public. In the words of John Sales, Gardens Adviser to the National Trust, 'In the development of gardening in the second half of the twentieth-century ... no garden writer has had a more profound influence' than her. She started writing about gardening in 1951 for *The Field* magazine and went on to write for *Punch*, *Amateur Gardening*, *Popular Gardening*, the *Journal* of the Royal Horticultural Society and many others.

Her writing has the directness of practical experience and observation, as though she had come straight from the border or the potting shed with earth still on her hands. Added to this, her way of describing her plants as dear friends, or sometimes as recalcitrant children, had great charm. Although never a journalist herself, this immediacy and directness must have been influenced by her many years working in the world of newspapers. Although most of her writing was about plants and their uses in the garden she wrote effectively on the more mundane but important gardening skills – making compost, propagation, labelling, organising the potting-shed and so forth. Much of what she described had particular relevance to her own gardening conditions. For example, because her own garden was on heavy clay she avoided walking on the soil as much as possible and most of her beds were narrow enough to be accessible from either side. Where this was impossible she made stepping stones, or even a narrow path, so that she could work among the plants without compacting the soil.

One of the great attractions to her readers was that she wrote chiefly about her own experiences at East Lambrook Manor – a garden they found it easy to visualise and could visit themselves. Here they saw the reality of what she preached and discovered things that gave them ideas for their own garden.

The following is a complete list of all her books, with their dates of first publication. With the exception of *An All the Year Garden* and *Gardening on Clay and Lime*, they are all in print.

We Made a Garden (1956)
An All the Year Garden (1958)
Cottage Garden Flowers (1961)
Ground Cover Plants (1964)
Gardening in the Shade (1964)
A Flower for Every Day (1965)
Carefree Gardening (1966)
Gardening on Clay and Lime (1970)

Index

Acaena buchananii 74
  microphylla 74
Acanthus mollis 63
Acer capillipes 55
  platanoides 'Goldsworth Purple' 55, 95, 109
  pseudoplatanus 'Leopoldii' 11
Achillea clavennae 87
  clypeolata (of gardens) 87
  fillipendula 'Gold Plate' 89
  millefolium 'Cerise Queen' 82
Aconitum lycoctonum vulparia 82
Actinidia kolomitka 38
Ajuga pyramidalis 73, 74
  p. 'Metallica Crispa' 113
  reptans 'Multicolor' 73
Akebia quinata 38
Alchemilla alpina 58
  mollis 58, 74
Allingham, Helen 20
Allium christophii 76
  moly 76
  rosenbachianum 76
  roseum 76
  sphaerocephalon 76
Alnus glutinosa 'Imperialis' 112
Amateur Gardening 21
Amelanchier canadensis 55, 111
Amory, Lady May 45
Anaphalis cinnamomea 87, 96
  margaritacea 87
  triplinervis 87
Anemone hupehensis 93
  h. 'Splendens' 93
  × *hybrida* 'Honorine Jobert' (syn. *A.* × *h.* 'Alba') 93
  × *h.* 'Luise Uhink' 93
  × *h.* 'Struttgardia' 93
  narcissiflora 111
  vulparia 93
Angelica archangelica 80
Aquilegia 'Hensol Harebell' 67
  canadensis 48
  vulgaris 'Munstead White' 67
Armeria maritima 75
  m. 'Alba' 75

m. 'Bee's Ruby' 75
Artemisia absinthium 86
  a. 'Lambrook Silver' 82, 86, 96, 99
  arborescens 'Faith Raven' 109
  canescens (of gardens) 86
  gracilis 110
  ludoviciana 86
  l. incompta (syn. *A. discolor*) 110
  pedemontana 86
  stelleriana 86
  tridentata 110
Arum italicum marmoratum (syn. *A.i. pictum*) 64
Aster × *frikartii* 96
  × *f.* 'Wunder von Staffa' 97
  lateriflorus 'Horizontalis' 97
  macrophyllus 97
  novi-belgii 'Climax' 97
  sedifolius nanus 97
  tongolensis 'Napsbury' 97
  tradenscantii 97, 113
Astrantia carniolica 77
  c. rubra 77
  major 77
  m. 'Shaggy' 77
  maxima 77
Atriplex hortensis rubra 92

Ballota pseudodictamnus 74, 110
Bellis perennis 'Dresden China' 70
  p. 'Prolifera'/'Hen and Chicken' 70
  p. 'Rob Roy' 70
Bergenia 'Ballawley' 64
  cordifolia 'Purpurea' 64
  purpurascens 54, 56, 64
  × *schmidtii* 42, 63
Birket Foster, Henry 20
Blickling Hall 15
Bowles, E. A. 27, 28, 53, 61, 85
Boyd-Carpenter, Francis and Nina 103
Boyd-Carpenter, Henry 2, 7, 23, 102, 104
Brachyglottis greyi 86, 110
  laxifolia 86
  monroi (syn. *Senecio monroi*) 86, 98
Britton, Nellie 45, 46
Brown, Jane 29

Brympton d'Evercy 43
Buddleja alternifolia 70
   'Lochinch' 38
Bupleurum angulosum 112
   fruticosum 58
Butt, Walter 53

Calamintha nepeta nepeta (syn. C. nepetoides) 98
Caltha palustris 'Flore Pleno' 65
Campanula 'Burghaltii' 80
   alliariifolia 80
   carpatica 35, 80
   glomerata 73, 75
   isophylla 81
   lactiflora 80, 109
   l. 'Pouffe' 109
   latifolia 'Lodden Anna' 80
   l. macrantha 80
   latiloba 80
   persicifolia 80
   p. alba 80
   p. planiflora 'Coronata' 80
   p. p. alba 80
   portenschlagiana 35, 74
   poscharskyana 74, 80
Cardamine pratensis 'Flore Pleno' 65
Carex pendula 95
Carpenteria californica 48
Ceanothus 'Burkwoodii' 38
   × veitchianus 37, 76
Centaurea cineraria cineraria (syn. C. gymnocarpa) 82
   montana 42
Cerastium tomentosum 73
Ceratostigma plumbaginoides 35
Cercis siliquastrum 75
   s. 'Alba' 112
Chaemaecyparis lawsoniana 'Fletcheri' 39
Cheiranthus cheiri 66
   c. 'Bloody Warrior' 66
   c. 'Harpur Crewe' 66
Chevithorne Barton 45
Choisya ternata 38, 55
Chrysanthemum 'Emperor of China' 96
   'Innocence' 96
   'Wedding Day' 96
Cimicifuga racemosa 97
   r. cordifolia 97
   ramosa 98
   simplex 'White Pearl' 97
Cistus hirsutus psilosepalus 111

Clematis 'Alba Luxurians' 84
   alpina 38
   armandii 84
   chrysocoma 38
   cirrhosa balearica 38, 58
   'Comtesse de Bouchaud' 85
   'Countess of Onslow' 93
   'Duchess of Edinburgh' 112
   'Etoile Violette' 85
   flammula 38
   'Henryi' 38
   heracleifolia 93
   h. davidiana 84
   × jackmanii 21, 37, 109
   × jouiniana 'Mrs. Robert Brydon' 109
   × j. 'Praecox' 100
   'Kermesina' 85
   'Lady Northcliffe' 85
   macropetala 38
   m. 'Markham's Pink' 38
   'Margot Koster' 112
   'Miss Bateman' 109
   montana 'Elizabeth' 109
   'Perle d'Azur' 38, 85, 110
   rehderiana 84, 85, 93
   tangutica 84, 85
   tibetana vernayi L S & E 13342 84
   'Ville de Lyon' 84
Clive, Violet 43
Cobaea scandens 38
Colchicum byzantinum 18
Colour Schemes for the Flower Garden (Gertrude Jekyll) 26
Conium maculatum 28
Convolvulus althaeoides 110
   cneorum 38
Cornus canadensis 41
   kousa chinensis 55
   mas 'Variegata' 111
Coronilla glauca 38, 113
   g. 'Variegata' 113
Corydalis solida 42
Corylus maxima 'Purpurea' 89
Cotoneaster horizontalis 45
   lacteus 100
Cottage Garden Magazine, The 21
Cottage gardens; history of 15
Crocosmia 'Solfaterre' 65
   paniculata (syn. Curtonus paniculatus) 98
   pottsii 98
Crocus tommasinianus albus 111
Crowe, Dame Sylvia 14, 43, 44

Cyclamen coum 54
  c. 'Atkinsii' 54
  c. caucasicum (*C. ibericum*) 54
  hederifolium 54
  repandum 54
Cynara cardunculus 98, 95, 109
  scolymus 87

Dactylorhiza elata 41
  foliosa 41
Daphne arbuscula 41
  cneorum 35, 41
  collina 41
  laureola 58
Delphinium 'Alice Artindale' 47, 109
Dianthus 'Brympton Red' 75
  caryophyllus 16
  gratianopolitanus 40, 77
  g. 'Double Cheddar' 77
  'Thomas' 75
Dicentra spectabilis 28

East Lambrook Manor; decorating of 9
East Lambrook Manor; history of 8
Eastwood, Dorothea 12
Education of a Gardener (Russell Page) 15
Enclosures Acts 19
English Flower Garden, The (William Robinson) 24, 25
Encyclopaedia of Gardening (John Claudius Loudon) 21
Epigaea asiatica 41
Erigeron 'Charity' 71
  glaucus 70
  multiradiatus 70
  philadelphicus 70, 73
  'Quakeress' 70
  speciosus macranthus (syn. *E. mesa-grande*) 70
Eryngium alpinum 109
  bourgatii 109
  giganteum 85
Erythronium californicum 66
  dens-canis 66
  tuolumnense 66
Euonymus fortunei 'Silver Queen' 55
  f. radicans 55
Euphorbia amygdaloides robbiae 62
  characias 62
  c. wulfenii 58, 62, 109
  c. w. 'Lambrook Gold' 62
  c. w. sibthorpii 62

  coralloides 63
  cyparissias 63
  dulcis 63, 98
  hyberna 62
  lathyrus 84
  mellifera 58, 62
  myrsinites 63
  pilosa 90
  polychroma 62, 63
  p. 'Major' (syn. *E. pilosa* 'Major') 63
  portlandica 63
  rigida 63
  sikkimensis 62

Farrand, Beatrix 49
× *Fatshedera lizei* 54
Fatsia japonica 21
Filipendula palmata 74
  vulgaris 74
Finnis, Valerie 9
Fish, Walter 6, 7, 8, 32, 33
Five Hundred Pointes of Good Husbandrie (Thomas Tusser) 18
'Florists'' flowers 18
Forsythia ovata 38
Fragaria 'Baron Solemacher' 74
  vesca 'Plymouth Strawberry' 74
  v. monophylla 74
  v. semperflorens (syn. *F. alpina*) 74
Fritillaria imperialis 18, 27
  meleagris 18, 66
  m. 'Poseidon' 65
Fuchsia magellanica 11
  'Mrs Popple' 35

Galanthus elwesii 54
  gracilis 54
  'Ophelia' 53
  plicatus byzantinus 54
Galium odoratum 75
Galtonia princeps 112
Garden Design 14
Garden Magazine, The 21
Gardener's Magazine, The 21
'Gardening with Walter' (*Punch* magazine) 5
Gardens; style in 1930s 12
Garrya elliptica 48, 83
Gentiana 'Inverleith' 46
  × *macaulayi* 46
  sino-ornata 46

Geranium delavayi 78
　endressii 40, 78, 109
　e. 'Wargrave Pink' 78
　himalayense 'Gravetye' 78
　ibericum 28, 78
　macrorrhizum 45, 56, 79
　m. album 79
　× *magnificum* (syn. *G. ibericum pla-typetalum*) 78
　malviflorum 79
　nodosum 79
　× *oxonianum* 'A. T. Johnson' 79
　× *o.* 'Claridge Druce' 79
　× *o.* 'Rose Clair' 79
　palmatum 78
　phaeum 79
　p. album 79
　pratense 77
　p. 'Plenum Violaceum' 30, 77
　p. 'Striatum' 78
　psilostemon 25, 78
　reflexum 79, 108
　renardii 79
　× *riversleaianum* 'Russell Prichard' 79
　robertianum 'Celtic White' 111
　sanguineum 79
　s. album 111
　s. striatum 74, 79
　sylvaticum 78
　s. album 111
　viscosissimum 78
　wallichianum 'Buxton's Variety' 79
Gertrude Jekyll on Gardening (Penelope Hobhouse) 27
Gladiolus communis byzantinus 76

Haddon, Norman 58
Hadfield, Miles 24
Hebe 'Spender's Seedling' 55
　cupressoides 100
Hedera helix 'Parsley Crested' 55
Helianthemum 'Wisley Pink' 110
Helichrysum ambiguum 110
　fontanesii 110
　italicum (syn. *H. angustifolium*) 87, 110
　sibthorpii 110
　splendidum 87
　stoechas 110
　s. barrelieri 56, 96
Helleborus argutifolius (syn. *H. lividus corsicus*) 58, 62
　cyclophyllus 58

　foetidus 27
　f. 'Italian form' 58
　'Greenland' 112
　lividus 58
Helleborus niger 28, 57
　n. macranthus 57
　odorus 57, 58
　orientalis abchasicus 57
　o. atrorubens 57
　o. guttatus 57
　o. kochii 57
　o. olympicus 57
　purpurascens 58
　× *sternii* 58
　torquatus (of gardens) 58
　viridis 58
Helychrysum splendidum 82
Hesperis matronalis alba double form 72, 113
Hidcote 15, 22
Hieracium aurantiacum 73
History of British Gardening, A (Miles Hadfield) 24
Hobhouse, Penelope 27
Horticultural Journal, The 21
Hosta fortunei 'Albopicta' 64
　lancifolia 70
　sieboldiana 70
　s. elegans 70
Houttuynia cordata 90
Hydrangea aspera villosa 100
　involucrata 'Hortensis' 100
　macrophylla 'Mariesii' 99, 100
　petiolaris 100
　serrata 'Grayswood' 99

Iris 'Paper Moon' 82
　bucharica 66
　cristata 46
　ensata 41
　foetidissima 58
　graeberiana 66
　histrioides sophensis 54
　magnifica 66
　orientalis 69
　pallida 'Argentea Variegata' 69
　p. 'Aurea Variegata' 69
　p. 'Variegata' 109
　pumila 66
　setosa 69
　sibirica 'Eric the Red' 69
　s. 'Snow Queen' 69
　susiana 66

unguicularis alba 54
 u. angustifolia 54

Jasminum officinale 37
Jekyll, Gertrude 14, 22, 25, 26, 27, 64, 85
Johnson, G. W. 21
Johnston, Lawrence 15, 22

Kerria japonica 21
 j. 'Picta' 95
Kirengeshoma palmata 46
Kniphofia 'Brimstone' 94
 caulescens 95
 galpini 95
 'Gold Else' 95
 'Little Maid' 113
 'Maid of Orleans' 94, 95
 'Modesta' 95
 northiae 94
 'Prince Igor' 47, 95
 rooperi 95, 96
 'Samuel's Sensation' 95
 thompsonii snowdenii 95
 triangularis (syn. *K. galpinii*) 95
 'Wrexham Buttercup' 94
Knole 29

Lamium galeobdolon 'Variegatum' 56, 64
Lane Fox, Robin 30, 52
Lathyrus latifolius 45, 67
 vernus alboroseus 67
Lavandula viridis 113
Leucanthemella serotina (syn. *Chrysanthemum uliginosum*) 42, 96
Ligustrum ovalifolium 'Argenteum' 85
Lilium candidum 16
 martagon 16
Lindsay, Norah 10, 15
Lindsay, Nancy 15
Linum narbonense 109
Liriope muscari 'Alba' 111
Lobelia cardinalis 90
 fulgens 63, 90
 syphilitica 90
 × *vedrariensis* 90
Lonicera japonica 'Halliana' 110
 nitida 34, 42
Loudon, John Claudius 21
Lychnis chalcedonica 16, 73
 coronaria 73
 flos-jovis 73

viscaria 'Spendens Plena' 71, 73
 × *walkeri* 'Abbotswood Rose' 73
Lysimachia ciliata 94
 clethroides 84, 93, 94
 ephemerum 94
 leschenaultii 94
 nummularia 94
 punctata 94
 vulgaris 94

Macleod, Dawn 3
Magnolia grandiflora 48
 g. 'Exmouth' 55, 78
 × *soulangeana* 111, 112
 stellata 55, 111
Mahonia aquifolium 11
 nervosa 38
Malva alcea fastigiata 100
Manual of Cottage Gardening, The (John Claudius Loudon) 21
Meconopsis betonicifolia 41
 cambrica 64
Mertensia virginica 48, 67
Mitella breweri 65
Monarda 'Cambridge Scarlet' 91
 didyma 91
 'Snow White' 91
Mottisfont Abbey 15
Myddleton House 27
Myosotis alpestris 64

Narcissi 'Queen Anne's Double' 59
 poeticus 'Flore Pleno' 59
 p. recurvus 59
National Trust, The 12
Nectaroscordum siculum 76
Nepeta × *faassenii* 71
 nervosa 71
 'Six Hills Giant' 71
 'Souvenir d'André Chaudron' 71
Nerine bowdenii 99
Nicolson, Harold 10, 14, 29
Northcliffe, Lord 4, 5, 6
Norton, Andrew and Dodo 104

Olearia moschata 110
Omphalodes cappadocica 66, 110
 luciliae 46
 verna 66
Ornithogalum nutans 66
 umbellatum 18, 66
Oxalis articulata 40

Pachysandra terminalis 49
Paeonia cambessedesii 72
  delavayi lutea 109
  mlokosewitschii 71, 72
  officinalis 'Rubra Plena' 71
  peregrina 72
  tenuifolia 71
Page, Russell 15
Paradisi in Sole Paradisus Terrestris (John Parkinson) 18
Parkinson, John 18
Penstemon 'Alice Hindley' 81, 109
  'Andenken an Friedrich Hahn' (syn. *P.* 'Garnet') 81, 109
  barbatus 81
  'George Home' 81
  heterophyllus 81
  '*Hewell's Pink*' 81
  isophyllus 38, 81, 97
  'Myddelton Gem' 81
  'Pennington Gem' 81, 97
  'Schonholzeri' 81
  'Stapleford Gem' 81
Perovskia atriplicifolia 92
Phalaris arundinacea 'Aureovariegata' 75
Philadelphus 'Beauclerk' 69
Phlomis fruticosa 96, 109
  lanata 110
Phlox paniculata 89
  p. 'Leo Schlageter' 90
  p. alba 89
Photinia davidiana undulata (syn. *Stranvaesia d.u.*) 100
Physostegia virginiana 98
  v 'Summer Spire' 98
  v. 'Vivid' 98
Pimpinella major rosea 75
Platt, James 46, 47
Polemonium caeruleum 72
  carneum 72
  foliosissimum 73
  reptans 'Lambrook Manor' 73
  r 'Sapphire' 73
  × *richardsonii* 72
Polygonatum biflorum 65
  × *hybridum* 'Flore Pleno' 65
  × *h.* 'Variegatum' 65
Polygonum affine 92
  a. 'Darjeeling Red' 92
  amplexicaule 'Album' 84
  bistorta 93
  b. 'Superbum' 93

  capitatum 109
  cuspidatum 63
  vaccinifolium 93
Potentilla 'Etna' 69
  'Gibson's Scarlet' 69
  'Miss Willmott' 69
  recta pallida 69
Primula 'Bartimaeus' 59
  chionantha 60
  clarkei 60
  denticulata 60
  elatior meyeri 'Grandiflora' 59
  florindae 60
  forrestii 60
  × *juliana* 'Jill' 42
  marginata 60
  Polyanthus 'Barrowby Gem' 59
  'Bon Accord Gem' 59
  'Enchantress' 111
  'Guinevere' 111
  'Kinlough Beauty' 111
  'Madame de Pompadour' 60
  'Our Pat' 59
  'Prince Silverwings' 111
  'Salamander' 111
  'Tawny Port' 111
  Primrose 'Miss Massey' 111
  'Tipperary Purple' 111
  'Wanda' 59
  prolifera 60
  × *pubescens* 60
  pulverulenta 'Bartley Strain' 60
  rosea 60
  sieboldii 57
  vulgaris 'Alba Plena' 59
  v. 'Lilacina Plena' 59
  v. 'Marie Crousse' 59
Prunella 'Loveliness' 74
Prunus × *subhirtella* 'Autumnalis' 55, 69, 82, 112
Pulmonaria officinalis 65
  rubra 102
  r. 'Bowles' Red' 65
  saccharata argentea 65
  vallarsae 'Margery Fish' 65
Pyrus salificifolia 'Pendula' 85

Ranunculus aconitifolius 18
  a. 'Flore Pleno' 65
  asiaticus 18
Reiss, Phyllis 14, 43, 44, 45

Reynoutria japonica 93
  j. 'Variegata' 93
Rheum palmatum 27
Rhodiola rosea 17
Rhus typhina 100
Ribes laurifolium 58
  sanguineum 21
Robinson, William 14, 21, 22, 23, 25, 26, 72
Romneya coulteri 48
Roper, Lanning 5, 47, 48, 49
Rosa 'Alberic Barbier' 82
  'Albertine' 37, 82
  'Aloha' 109
  'American Pillar' 36, 37, 82, 109
  'Breeze Hill' 85
  brunonii 108
  'Chaplin's Pink' 39
  'Climbing Caroline Testout' 37
  'Climbing General McArthur' 37
  'Climbing Lady Hillingdon' 37, 39
  'Climbing Madame Abel Chatenay' 37
  'Climbing Madame Butterfly' 38
  'Climbing Ophelia' 37
  'Complicata' 84
  'Cupid' 39
  'Dorothy Perkins' 11, 82
  'Dr van Fleet' 83
  eglanteria 21
  filipes 'Kiftsgate' 85, 107
  'Frau Karl Druschki' 82
  'Frensham' 82, 91
  'Fru Dagmar Hastrup' 83
  gallica 16
  'George Dickson' 82
  'Gloire de Dijon' 37, 39
  'Goldfinch' 109
  'Great Maiden's Blush' 11, 21, 81
  'Guinée' 83
  'Hugh Dickson' 82
  'Iceberg' 82
  × *jacksonii* 'Max Graf' 83
  'Little White Pet' 86
  macrantha 83
  m. 'Daisy Hill' 83
  m. 'Raubritter' 83
  'Madame Abel Chatenay' 83
  'Magenta' 82
  'Mermaid' 109
  'Mrs John Laing' 82
  'New Dawn' 82, 85
  × *odorata* 'Mutabilis' 83
  'Paul's Perpetual White' 109

  'Paul's Scarlet Climber' 37, 39, 109
  'Paulii' 83
  'Radium' 97
  'Rambling Rector' 107
  'Rosemary Rose' 81, 83
  'Roseraie de l'Haÿ' 71
  'Sander's White Rambler' 82
  'Schneelicht' 83
  'Sterling Silver' 82
  'Viridiflora' 83, 112
  wichuraiana 82
  'William Lobb' 78
  'Zepherine Drouhin' 38, 83
Rubus Tridel 38
Rudbeckia fulgida sullivantii 'Goldsturm' 82

Sackville-West, Vita 10, 14, 22, 29, 30, 31
Sales John 114
Salvia argentea 98, 110
  azurea 91
  candelabra 92
  grahamii 92
  haemotodes 91
  patens 91
  pratensis 91
  sclarea turkestanica 82, 91
  uliginosa 91
Sanguinaria canadensis 48
Santolina pinnata neapolitana 87
  p. n. 'Sulphurea' 87
Saponaria officinalis 11
  o. 'Rosea Plena' 73
Savill Garden 14, 78
Savill, Col. Eric 14
Saxifraga × *urbium* 74
Schizostylis coccinea 'Mrs Hegarty' 98
Scott-James, Anne 53
Scutellaria incana 73
  i. parvifolia 98
Sedum 'Autumn Joy' 92
  'Ruby Glow' 92
  telephium 92
  t. 'Munstead Dark Red' 92
  t. maximum 109
  t. m. 'Atropurpureum' 92, 109
Selinum tenuifolium 75
Senecio bicolor cineraria 'Ramparts' 86
  b. c. 'White Diamond' 86
  scandens 38
Senecio vira-vira (syn. *S. leucostachys*) 38, 81, 86
Shizostylis coccinea 'Viscountess Byng' 98

Silene dioica 'Rosea Plena' 73
Sissinghurst Castle 14, 22, 29, 30
× *Solidaster* 'Lemore' 89, 91
Somerset, Margery's thoughts on; 9
Stachys byzantina 74
   b. 'Silver Carpet' 74, 110
Stauntonia hexaphylla 84
Story of Gardening, The; Richardson Wright
   12
Story of our Gardening, The; Dorothea East-
wood 12
Suburban Gardener, The 21

Tanacetum macrophyllum 96
   parthenium 'White Bonnet' 109
   p. aureum 96
Teucrium fruticans 76
Thalictrum delavayi 99
Thomas, Graham Stuart 52
Tintinhull 14, 43, 44
Trachycarpus fortunei 112
Tradescantia virginiana 19
Tricyrtis formosana Stolonifera group (syn.
T. stolonifera) 99
   hirta 99
   h. alba 99
   latifolia 99
   macropoda 99
Tropaeolum speciosum 45
Turner, William 18
Tusser, Thomas 18

Veratrum album 65
   nigrum 65
   viride 65, 112

Verbascum bombyciferum 56, 87
   rotundifolium haenseleri 87
Verbena rigida 92
Veronica filiformis 73
   gentianoides 63
Viburnum farreri 84
Vinca difformis 56
   major hirsuta 112
   minor 53, 56
   m. alba 53
   m. 'Argenteo-variegata' 53
   m. atropurpurea 53
   m. 'Azurea Flore Pleno' 53
   m. 'La Grave' 53, 56
   m. 'Multiplex' 53
Viola 'Admiral Avellan' 61
   biflora 61
   'Bowles' Black' 61
   'Coeur d'Alsace' 61
   cornuta 61, 70, 93
   'Duchesse de Parme' 61
   'John Raddenburg' 61
   labradorica 45
   l. purpurea 61
   'Marie Louise' 61
   pensylvanica 61
   'Red Queen' 61
   'Swanley White' 61
Vita's Other World (Jane Brown) 29

Whitsey, Fred 105
Wild Garden, The (William Robinson)
24
Willmott, Ellen 85
Wright, Richardson 12